PREVAIL

Tackling Troubled Times In The Words Of
Olympic Peninsula Authors

PREVAIL

Tackling Troubled Times In The Words Of
Olympic Peninsula Authors

COPYRIGHT ©2020 by Olympic Peninsula Authors.

All Rights Reserved. No part of this book may be used or reproduced in any manner whatsoever without the written permission of the author(s) except in the case of brief quotations for critical articles or reviews.

The authors in this anthology are the sole copyright owners of their individual works and retain all rights except for those expressly granted to Olympic Peninsula Authors and/or H3 Press.

- Compiled and edited by Linda B. Myers and Heidi Hans
- Cover design by Roslyn McFarland with Far Lands Publishing
- Interior design by Heidi Hansen

Published by H3 Press, PO Box 312, Carlsborg, WA 98324
ISBN: 978-0998252698

Acknowledgement is made for permission to publish:

© 1995-2020 Jan Thatcher Adams, M.D., All rights reserved.
© 2014-2020 Gordon Anderson, All rights reserved.
© 2020 Craig Andrews, All rights reserved.
© 2020 Jeri Bidinger, All rights reserved.
© 2020 Gary E. Bullock, All rights reserved.
© 2020 Lauralee DeLuca, All rights reserved.
© 2020 Eric Dieterle, All rights reserved.
© 2020 Judith R. Duncan, All rights reserved.
© 2020 Jon Eekhoff, All rights reserved.
© 2020 Joan Enoch, M.D., All rights reserved.
© 2020 Susan Erickson, All rights reserved.
© 2016-2020 Heidi Hansen, All rights reserved.
© 2020 Samantha Hines, All rights reserved.
© 2020 Derek Huntingdon, All rights reserved.
© 2020 Katherine See Kennedy, All rights reserved.
© 2020 Al Kitching, All rights reserved.
© 2016-2020 Dianne L. Knox, All rights reserved.
© 2020 Pamela S. Kuhlmann, All rights reserved.
© 2020 Jon Langdon, All rights reserved.
© 2020 Eva McGinnis, All rights reserved.
© 2020 Melee McGuire, All rights reserved.
© 2020 Terry Moore, All rights reserved.
© 2016-2020 Linda B. Myers, All rights reserved.
© 2020 John Norgord, All rights reserved.
© 2020 Terry Sager, All rights reserved.
© 2020 Sarah Shepard, All rights reserved.
© 2020 Steve Valadez All rights reserved.
© 2020 Louise Lenahan Wallace, All rights reserved.

DEDICATION

Washington's Olympic Peninsula provides a backdrop of solace and inspiration for all who live here. This volume is dedicated to the people of the Peninsula as we take strength from our wilderness and forge pathways through troubled times.

CONTENTS

Gary E. Bullock 2
Eva McGinnis 4
Sarah Shepard 16
Katherine See Kennedy 23
Eric Dieterle 37
Jon Langdon 40
Linda B. Myers 58
Judith R. Duncan 72
Jeri Bidinger 74
Gordon Anderson 82
Craig Andrews 93
John Norgord 102
Lauralee DeLuca 108
Steven Valadez 112
Jon Eekhoff 115
Derek Huntington 127
Susan Erickson 131
Samantha Hines 135
Dianne L. Knox 140
Louise Lenahan Wallace 148
Pamela S. Kuhlmann 152
Joan Enoch, M.D. 161
Melee McGuire 171
Terry Sager 183
Al Kitching 191
Heidi Hansen 198
Jan Thatcher Adams, M.D. 209
Terry L. Moore 222

PREVAIL

Tackling Troubled Times In The Words Of
Olympic Peninsula Authors

2020 has thrown curves at us all, making everyone confront situations never expected, follow surprising detours, learn sudden lessons on how to prevail during unsettled times. The twenty-eight Olympic Peninsula authors in this collection have stepped up with stories, poems, memoirs, and essays about prevailing today, in the past, or in the future. You'll find humor, pathos, personal reflections, a sense of community, and maybe a touch of hope as we soldier on together.

Gary E. Bullock

Gary lived the Alaska Dream for thirty-five years. He retired to the Olympic Peninsula in 2012 after a thirty-seven-year firefighting career and twenty-two years as University of Alaska adjunct faculty.

Gary's writing also includes haiku and essays. His writing celebrates and echoes his love of birds and nature. An avid birder he has a life list of over five hundred species.

Twice a cancer survivor, and a U.S. Air Force veteran, he lives in a little slice of paradise with his wife Lee, and Robin the Wonder Dog.

Contact Gary at gbullockak@hotmail.com

IN THE WORDS OF GARY E. BULLOCK

STOPPING BY COSTCO ON A COVID EVENING

(With apologies to Robert Frost)

Whose eyes are those, I think I know,
I think it must be Neighbor Joe.
Blue mask and gloves, dressed very smart,
I'm sure it's him; not really though.

No room to steer this big red cart,
we must maintain six feet apart.
Back off! Back up! You're too close, Dude!
Be still, this tremble in my heart.

Look there, in line, no mask - so rude,
paper goods piled high, but no food.
A one-case limit, there's the sign.
Just saw him sneeze, oh God, we're screwed!

Yes, we should buy a box of wine
to drink with takeout, bought online,
and fit it all inside the Jeep.
Sure hope their chef's still feeling fine.

This mask, it makes my left eye weep,
for I have fears my health won't keep,
and unseen smiles to dream in sleep,
and unseen smiles to dream in sleep.

Eva McGinnis

Writing and acts of kindness have been wonderfully linked in my life; even pointing the way to the man I would marry. We were in college when my vision was temporarily impaired during finals week. Though he had his own assignments, he stayed up all night and typed my essays for my English classes. We married the following summer and have recently reached our fifty year mark. We enjoy our lives in Port Angeles after careers in academic and non-profit worlds. We both love photography, creating glass art, taking our inspiration from nature. We've had joint photos and poems at the Sequim Art Show (Fluidity) online in 2020. I facilitate a writing group in my neighborhood.

After completing a certificate program in Poetry at the UW, two books of my poetry have been published: *Wings to my Breath* and *At the Edge of the Earth* and several works appear in literary books, including *In the Words of Olympic Peninsula Authors Vols 2 & 3, Tidepools 2016, 2017 & 2020, Rainshadow Poetry Anthology, Wild Willow Women's Anthology Project, Seattle Poems by Seattle Poets Anthology, Woman as Hero Anthology, A Mother's Touch, Spindrift '93, '94 & '95.*

Contact Eva at Evapoet@mcginnishome.org

NOBODY EXPECTS
THE SPANISH INQUISITION

If you were a fan of the British comedy troupe Monty Python's Flying Circus in the 1970s and 1980s, you would recognize their famous punchline, *"Nobody expects the Spanish Inquisition."* Over the years, my husband and I have used it as our humor code for the surprise we felt whenever the unexpected suddenly arrived in our lives. We used it when we lost electricity during winter storms, when cutbacks left me without a job and even when I got a rare speeding ticket. There was that unexpected *Spanish Inquisition*, so outrageously out of context that we would chuckle and eventually laugh at whatever surreal situation we found ourselves in. We've even used it when the absurd politics of the world surprised us.

The wonder is that this crazy phrase still works today, though fewer people understand or remember the reference. Since the COVID-19 shutdown of March 2020, we have certainly experienced surreal tests of our humor-coping skills in dealing with the unexpected. In fact, these unusual incidences have become so ubiquitous that the COVID-19 pandemic has become more of a backdrop, a masked given, when dealing with even more pressing issues.

Our normally healthy friends have had hospitalizations; good drivers have been involved in automobile accidents; and my own careful husband recently fell off a ladder while painting the side of our house. There was the rush to the ER with its COVID-19 backdrop – I couldn't accompany him inside to check for broken bones (none were found) and get facial stitches and staples. Then there was the trip to the Tacoma area for dental and orthodontic appointments for the chipped teeth and fractures in gums (COVID-19 backdrop – got temperature checks everywhere we went). On the positive side, there were many helpful angel friends and neighbors smoothing our way with their compassion and loving help.

We both passed the emergency action stage of this accident into the humor stage within a day. I consoled my husband with, "It's the first time, honey, that you look better with a mask than without." A neighbor recommended that he leave the "ladder wrestling" to the professionals. The jokes came so quickly that my husband asked for a respite from them, "until it didn't hurt to laugh." But I could tell by the smile in his eyes that inside he was okay. It wasn't long before we both looked at each other and said, "No one expects the Spanish Inquisition."

However, when there have been more serious situations which we could not find the humor in, we have relied on two other mantras to get us through. The first is "This too shall pass." In this constantly changing world, it's a way to accept what we cannot change and be grateful for what we do have and can control, like our own feelings and reactions. I have used this when our daughter called from California with an injury which couldn't get treated because the hospitals were on COVID-19 closures. I also repeated "this too shall pass" in the time of fires and dangerous air quality in the Bay area, where she lives. I couple this mantra with affirmative prayer that focuses on gratitude for what is going right and staying in the NOW moment, where we are all safe. I trust that we are in God's hands. I meditate in mindfulness. These have been steadying strategies for me.

The second resilience mantra that I use is "Everything matters, but not very much." I acknowledge whatever the situation is and that it matters. But then I pivot to the bigger picture.

I have been blessed with seven decades of life experiences. They have given me a broader perspective that I didn't have in my twenties when I felt that I needed to be so firmly in charge. I felt then that everything mattered, passionately. This tongue-in-check affirmation works for softening differences of opinion, which seem so important when I'm in the midst of them. Too many times I have wasted energy on things that I now don't care about. In the moment, it matters, but ultimately – not very much.

An example of looking at things from what really matters came with the COVID-19 restrictions. We had been planning our fiftieth wedding anniversary celebration for months, complete with renewal of vows and a big dinner party afterwards. We had secured the venues, entertainment and caterer, and sent out invitations. Everything except for ordering the cake was complete. A dear friend had even started pre-baking and freezing the biscuits she was contributing to the dinner. When the lockdown came in March, we thought that by June we all would surely be free of the virus. But as the weeks went by, it became apparent that no parties were happening in June or all summer, and we cancelled all our plans. We were disappointed, but taken in the context of what so many others were going through, health-wise and financially, we felt ours was a minor inconvenience. Taken in the big picture view of "everything matters, but not very much," we celebrated being happily married and in good health when the day came, quietly and in great gratitude. We even got an unexpected gift when we were in the planning stage: we reconnected with friends we had lost touch with for forty-five years, who had been part of our wedding party. Now we Zoom with them regularly and our hearts are full. And our anniversary party can be rescheduled when it is safe. Perhaps celebrating fifty-five years? Everything matters (in the moment), but not very much (in the long run).

So, how have I changed and how am I coping?

The unexpected events challenge me to be more flexible and integrate change gracefully into my life. I don't let uncertainty about the future become the fear virus. I acknowledge "what is" but then move into actions that give my life meaning. Thinking in the bigger picture has softened my need to be in control, and that has brought a greater awareness of the need for kindness and caring for others into the forefront.

Where there are differences between people, I try to find areas of commonality, because if I listen long enough there is always something that I can find for us to agree upon, if only our love of our families, nature, or art. These bonds of mutual interest are even more important in these challenging times when divisiveness seems to be in vogue. Besides, they challenge me to become a more compassionate human being. In these times, I welcome opportunities to be of service, like organizing our neighbors to send greeting cards to someone in a long-term care facility, who was unable to leave her small room. More than ever, I see that small things and gestures do matter, providing a helping hand or an encouragement or a silly joke, even if I can't give hugs. In the end, I can laugh at myself, choose JOY in my life no matter what the circumstances, and even anticipate that I will encounter and prevail over "the Spanish Inquisition" moments in my life.

INOCULATION FOR RESILIENCE

I was teaching a workshop for Western Washington University to a group of harried state employees on new federal regulations in the 1990s. At break time, they were commiserating about how difficult and stressful their work was and how they resented all these changes. Except for one older gentleman, who was relaxed and smiled throughout the workshop. He seemed to be the only one who was taking the changes in stride. So I asked him about his positive attitude. His reply to the whole group was a surprise.

"This job, sitting at a desk and talking to people is not stressful for me. What was difficult was escaping from Vietnam, as the war raged around us. My brother and I were on one of the last boats out of the country. I saw other people die, and I expected that I would as well. That was stressful! This is easy. I am happy to have this job." His resilient attitude awakened the whole group to their privilege of working in safety and the relative insignificance of their complaints. His life-harrowing experiences had put the rest of his life into perspective. He found joy, where others found stress.

I have considered his attitude recently when reading about and witnessing people struggling with the COVID-19 pandemic, the economic fallout and the hardships many are undergoing, including the exposure of all the systemic inequities that have been laid bare. And I have wondered how to keep the positive perspective and not be stressed into complaining and commiserating.

What skills have I developed to deal with the challenges that are inevitable in every lifetime?

In the last few months, I have realized that I too have been toughened up to be resilient, albeit second-hand. Growing up, my parents inoculated me against threats and unexpected situations with the stories of their survival in Poland in the midst of WWII, which took home, family and freedom away from them. While still in her teens, my mother was enslaved and taken for forced farm labor into Germany. My father was wounded and captured in an ambush during the Polish army evacuation and spent years as a prisoner of war under tortuous conditions.

When I asked them about the specific ways with which they had managed to stay alive, my mother said that her faith in God helped her to survive. My father's answer was more about grit and a steely resolve. "Don't let them get you" was his motto. He credited his fellow soldiers in keeping each other sane and alive.

What I realized early on was that no matter how difficult situations appeared in my life, they would never be as dire as what my parents had endured. My mother stood under a tree to "avoid" Allied airplanes as they sent bombs whistling down around her, not knowing that she and other farm laborers where not the enemy. She refused to go down into the bomb shelter with her captors. She embodied the strength of her convictions.

Compared to those terror-filled experiences, my problems have never been in the same league. I might not have always felt safe, but I also have not lived in the kind of fear my parents did during that war (and with their PTSD afterwards). Their courage and survival skills have powered my own resilience in crises and difficult times. I watched their courage and steadfastness, and learned to keep calm and be patient.

I have kept my wits about me when others panicked, like when there was a fire. At ten years old, I was the one to call the fire department (before there was a 911 system). When a classmate was injured, I handled the bloodied elbow till we could get help. And I voluntarily took all the first aid courses whenever offered in my work life, ready to be ready when needed.

My parents' deep wounds vaccinated me against the comparatively mild scratches that my life has given me, as I have been blessed to live in this country, even with all its flaws. When there have been unexpected disappointments in my life, my parents reminded me that millions of others lived in far worse situations. As a result, food was never wasted in our home, because there were other families going without. Clothes were passed down then shipped to family where cousins eagerly awaited them. We had the privilege of living in a single family house, small though it was, with only six of us, as compared to overcrowded conditions that my parents and I had experienced in Displaced Persons camps. In the US, my sisters and I had access to schools, which provided us with skills to create better lives. We have been free to worship as we please. We have never had to wear symbols on our clothes that identified our nationality or religion as my parents did during the Nazi occupation.

Whenever I was tempted to feel sorry for myself, my mother would admonish me to "go and help another, who doesn't have what you have." She taught me to realize that there would always be those with more and those with less than me. So my task has been to focus my energy on giving to those in need and being grateful for all my blessings. I learned that it's useless to be in judgement and silly to be jealous.

So today, I might have minor challenges with restrictions that we are experiencing during the COVID-19 pandemic, like keeping social distancing or wearing sweaty masks in the summer, but I am not in fear. Even the smoke-filled skies only block the sun temporarily. I have faith that we are all in the Divine Plan of the Creator and there's no use resisting and complaining about what we cannot change.

Through this early acceptance of challenging times and examples of great courage and generosity, I have a gritty determination and trust today that I too can survive anything. "This too shall pass" is one of my mantras. And I live knowing I am constantly adding to my store of resiliency. I know at my core that I am always being taken care of by the part of me that is eternally linked with the Divine. I have an incredible community of dear friends and family that look out for me at all times. I have been mightily blessed and I am grateful for this gift of LIFE, good health, and community. I have purpose, and I live in awe of each day as a gift. Happiness is my shield, and humor is my sanity. I choose to serve, love and enjoy life no matter what else is going on.

If my parents could transform their lives of misery to decent productive ones, I know that I can face my life challenges as well. And like the Vietnamese gentleman and my parents, I have a big picture perspective to embrace whatever else life has to offer, with compassion, faith and a smile.

NEVER SAW IT COMING?

In "War of the Worlds" fictional broadcast,
giant alien invaders were disabled
by the smallest of microbes,
for which they had no immunities.

So too the machinery of 2020 businesses
the ships of war, factories, institutions
schools, universities, parks and concerts
ground to a stop with fear of contagious virus.

Cracks and chasms opened in the structures,
by which time and worth were measured,
unequally swallowing the vulnerable and poor.
Lives lost or forever altered. No hugs at funerals.

But light also beamed through those openings
as parents and children rediscovered each other,
when they sought to work, study and live together.
As communities found their purpose in service.

New ways to communicate, to see each other,
alternatives to working in claustrophobic cubicles
recognition of essential workers, (that's everyone)
and glaring disparities in pay and working conditions.

Extended time, to take off the blinders of routine
and listen to each other's wounds and joys.
Quiet of slower pace, planting a garden,
Breathing in nature and rediscovering priorities.

Most of all, the light shed on Oneness
of all humanity and the living environment,
refusing fear and extending LOVE.

Sarah Shepard

Sarah Shepard has a Master of Fine Arts from Northwest Institute of Literary Arts on Whidby Island, Washington.

She has written a full-length memoir about her struggle to rescue her little boy from an austere community, called *Let The World Around Us Fade Away*. She is working on two young adult novels. One is about a young girl trying to solve her grandfather's murder called *The Hollywood Kid,* and the other, called *Tug*, is about a young girl from Sequim who steals a tugboat to save three Sudanese orphans. She has submitted several short stories about her childhood adventures with her Quaker Missionary family to magazines.

Contact Sarah at sarahshepard@yahoo.com

THE WALLS BETWEEN US

My room is dark. The blinds stay closed all day. I don't want my neighbors to look in and see my bedside toilet.

My room is my daughter Bethany's bedroom. She traded with me when the first nursing home coronavirus deaths were reported. Bethany is a caregiver in a nursing home. Two of her co-workers came down with the virus. Now she and her kids, Ben 10, and Anna, 7, sleep in the living room. My husband John stays in the bedroom we used to share in Bethany's home.

Months ago John moved me in with a bed, recliner, mini-trampoline, fan, fridge, hotplate, and a microwave. And closed my door for the last time. He knocks and leaves my food on a tray. We never see each other face to face, so I wear his t-shirt for his scent and the lemon oil he uses on his guitar.

John is the only one allowed to touch my things. But Ben sometimes sneaks little treats onto my tray. I can't sanitize powdered sugar donut holes. But I eat them, three of them, even though they've come from his sticky little hands.

I have Parkinson's and multiple lung diseases. Even in "normal" times my lungs are fragile. When smoke drifted over the Bay Area from the wildfires last summer I could barely breathe. I became too sick to walk.

My room feels crowded. For a while I paced like a caged animal. Now I try to use my time to pray, sing, reflect, forgive, think about what really matters. I listen to smooth Motown jazz. I write.

I also cry all the time. I cry at seven every night when New Yorkers clap for first responders. I cry when I see someone kind on the news. I cry for everyone who has died and for their families.

I look like Boo Radley in *To Kill A Mockingbird*. Frightfully pale, with my hair buzzed off because sponge bathing is all I can do with no running water. Dark half-moons bloom under my eyes. I need sun.

For exercise I jump on my mini trampoline. My family thought of everything. We always have.

I'm resigned. I don't feel sorry for myself because there is a kind of comfort in numbers. There are millions of families like ours: poor, multigenerational, multiracial, squeezed into very small apartments. This one is just trying to protect a grandmother.

A year and a half ago John and I moved from Sequim, Washington, to the San Francisco Bay Area. We lived in a hundred-year-old cabin on ten acres, surrounded by seventy-foot trees. Resting my head on his shoulder, we would study the dancing stars through the skylight and be lulled to sleep by the ripples of the creek in our backyard. We had a year's supply of food and a generator, prepared for the end of world as we know it. We had a glacier in the mountains behind us and the Strait of Juan de Fuca in front.

The view from my window now is a parking lot.

I left the cabin when Bethany's husband divorced her. Originally I moved in to take care of the children. Then John moved in to take care of me, with our two dogs in tow. It was fun being together. I grew up in a big family. My parents raised eight children, four of their own and four foster kids from the local juvenile hall. I was brought up to be other-centered. I'm not helping anyone.

My grandkids and I used to give the upstairs neighbor kids lots of snacks and a couple tablets to play with. Now they are very quiet, and I worry they don't have enough food. I never see their parents in the parking lot with bags of groceries. I never see them go out anymore.

My grandchildren, Ben and Anna, tap on the wall between our rooms. I respond with a little tap to show them I'm okay. Our own little jail talk. They giggle. They tap louder with their fists. I pound with my fists. The kids upstairs jump up and down on their floor, our ceiling, and scream. The house rattles as if in an earthquake. My grandbabies are now kicking the walls with their heels, squealing and screaming. I kick my walls with my heels and belt out a thunderous roar and it feels good. Really good.

I shout, "I love you!"

"I love you, Grandma!" they shout back. "I love you!"

WATTS 1965

It's fry-an-egg-on-the-sidewalk hot on our way home from the Watts Towers. My sister Zona and I are skipping, wearing matching neon capris, neon shirts, and flip-flops. She's ten, and I'm eleven. We're Quaker, White and from the suburbs about ninety miles from Watts. We're here for the summer and live with twelve people of all colors and religions in the Friends Freedom House to teach people to read so they can vote.

We pass kept lawns, freshly painted houses, and flowers lined up against picket fences. We reach our front porch and sit on the steps. Our Black neighbors believe in loving your neighbor as yourself and welcome us into their hearts and homes. But it doesn't mean people aren't hungry here.

"I'm hungry," I say.

Zona scratches her leg. "You're always hungry."

The dark sky and the smell of smoke and smog make me uneasy. California has four seasons - drought, fire, flood, and earthquake, and this sure seems like earthquake weather to me.

Laverne opens the screen door. She's Jewish, twenty-three, and has long curly red hair. "Who wants to go out for spaghetti?"

I want spaghetti. Laverne gets behind the wheel of her big station wagon. Zona and I pile in the back seat and immediately start to pat-a-cake.

I realize something's brewing in the streets. A group of Black men with weapons stand shoulder-to-shoulder blocking the crosswalk.

I shout at Laverne. "Don't stop! Don't stop!"

Laverne stops.

The men surround us, rock the car, smash the windows with crowbars and throw a huge wrench through the driver's side window, and hit Laverne in the head. She slumps onto the steering wheel, making the horn scream. We're screaming, too. We have shattered glass in our faces. Blood drips onto our neon clothes. Laverne's bleeding heavily. Lavern's out cold.

I jump over the front seat while the men still rock the car and shout at us and to each other. I push Laverne to the side with my feet. It takes every bit of strength I have. Zona climbs over and sits next to me. I can't see over the dashboard. I try to gun the gas pedal but I'm too small to reach it. I tell Zona to get on the floor and push the gas pedal, but nothing happens. I put the car in drive.

"Push the gas, now!" I say.

The car lurches, and the men spill out of the way. I get up on my knees to see.

We careen through stop signs and traffic lights and crowds.

Downtown store windows are smashed, and there are fires everywhere, and people are stealing, some running out of shops with big TVs. We are choking from toxic fumes. I tell Zona to hit the brakes when I see a white cop. He shouts, "Get the hell out of here!"

"We need a hospital!"

He points up a hill. A woman rushes behind him, cradling her baby. He spins and hits her in the face with his baton. The woman drops the baby before she falls. The baby hits the asphalt hard. I hear wailing as we flee. Not the baby's.

I will see this scene like a movie loop for the rest of my life.

The road is blocked by burning trash, tires, and brush. I make a U-turn back to our house. Our neighbors run to us. Mister Wayne tells us to get in the way back of Laverne's station wagon. Other neighbors carry Laverne there too. Miss Ricky applies bandages and covers Laverne with a blanket. "Get under the blanket," she says to us.

"She needs a doctor," I say as several Black friends pile into the front and back seats.

"Who would want to hurt small children because of the color of their skin?" Miss Ricky asks.

"Hmph," Mr. Wayne grunts. "We're going to the hospital, baby," he says to me.

Black men are patrolling the streets, starting checkpoints.

"Stay very still," Miss Ricky says. "And hush."

I'm afraid Laverne is dead. I can smell her blood and vomit.

Mister Wayne stops the car. I bite my lip and cover Zona with my arm.

I hear a voice. "Hey man, they shouldn't have smashed your car like that man."

"Don't I know it," Mister Wayne says.

I hear the passengers quietly pray. We are allowed to pass through.

Our neighbors learned to read that summer so they could vote. Our neighbors covered us with love and saved our lives.

Katherine See Kennedy

I am a retired attorney, journalist, and editor, having recently completed a Master's from the California Institute of Integral Studies in philosophy, cosmology, and consciousness. I have spent many years exploring spirituality, depth psychology, dreams, and mind/body connection.

In 2018, my husband and I moved into the Olympic Mountains east of Port Angeles and delight to waking up every morning face-to-face with Burnt Mountain, just around the corner from Hurricane Ridge, my favorite place in the whole world. I am grateful to have a neighborhood writing group to support each other's efforts which has awakened my dormant muse!

I hope that my poetry can contribute to increased ecological consciousness and transformation of the relationships between humans and the other-than-human world on which we depend.

Contact Katherine at katkennedy9048@olypen.com

THE PERFECT STORM

In the seventh anguished month of the virus,
she fights her desperate lungs for breath.
A silver-haired weaver, she had been
sliding her weft through windings of purple and green,
thinking about picking blueberries
for her grandchildren's breakfast
when a sudden chill hit,
and pain blossomed behind her eyes.
Now cytokine storms flood her bloodstream,
primal terror constricting her body.
A doctor wearing a tattered mask
kept in a paper bag between patients
leans into her deadly exhalations
with grim determination
as a refrigerated truck patiently waits
outside the eerily lit emergency room.

Across the street in the fading day,
a yellow-breasted warbler leaves his summer home
in a willow and alder thicket,
embarking on his annual migration
to a shaded coffee plantation in Mexico
where his kin have wintered since the beginning.
The tiny bird (the size of a small child's palm,
weighing less than a pat of butter)
makes the journey by night,
navigating by the stars,
and by the map encoded in his cells.

IN THE WORDS OF KATHERINE SEE KENNEDY

He is unaware of the monstrous orange firestorm
devouring the land to the south,
ignited by lightning and a backyard party game.
The drought-ravaged earth with its desiccated foliage
supplies endless tinder for the gluttonous wraith.
It exhales poisonous plumes of tar and creosote,
a black beast riding the jet stream over the blue globe,
capriciously swallowing an old woman's home,
leaving only her white picket fence.
It chases down entire families,
engulfs them with a merciless roar
as they try to flee in their cars.
Millions of foxes, rabbits, coyotes, deer, frogs,
are smoked out of their homes and burned alive.

The bird flies into the trusted dark,
down the coasts of Oregon and California.
But the smoky night sky obscures his sidereal coordinates,
And he loses for the first time
the winged intelligence of his body,
the constancy of moon and stars.
He finally veers from the ancestral route,
seeking with his beady black eyes
a place to rest, a leafy, moist refuge
where bugs and seeds and red berries
offer themselves to the avian pilgrim.
Landing, he finds a lifeless expanse of arid earth,
shorelines littered with the dried skeletons of fish.

PREVAIL

He takes to the sky again,
propelled by the ancestral promise,
but finds only wasteland below.
His lungs blacken as his muscles begin to weaken.

At midnight they fall,
the human into an abyss of endless darkness,
the bird into a dry arroyo in New Mexico —
two creatures faithful to the impulse of life,
tumbling to earth.

This is the way the world is undone:
One singular life at a time.

IN THE WORDS OF KATHERINE SEE KENNEDY

TWO KINDS OF COURAGE

"As soon as you trust yourself, you will know how to live."
--Johann Wolfgang von Goethe

What is this darkness
that stalks me, unbidden,
prying open the door
looking for the one in hiding?
Who is it that holds me hostage
for refusing to deliver
the fragile holiness of my life?

So many are hypnotized
to trust the words that make them small,
sign contracts surrendering their souls
for the promise of lounging safely through life.
After seven decades, finally I ask
the questions long silenced
for fear of what the answers would require.

At the mouth of the Tasman Sea
on a radiant October dawn,
I stand unguarded, alone on the deck.
Sprays of white water fan over my body,
rainbows shining in filigreed arcs
as the bow descends into deep troughs,
climbs the wall of the swell, then plunges again.

PREVAIL

What is this joy,
this augery of confidence
in the easy rise and fall of a body,
if not the consort of shadow,
welcomed to the passage of my life?
The heart constricts with terror of drowning,
but the truth is: the dark, rolling sea will hold you up.

There are two kinds of courage,
and only one leads to freedom:
The courage to endure —
to cling to the wheel through tumultuous waters
as if your life depended on it —
and the courage to let go,
leaping into unknown depths with arms flung wide.

IN THE WORDS OF KATHERINE SEE KENNEDY

CROSSING THE DIVIDE

The land remembers gray against blue,
butchery of brother by brother,
leaving a wreckage of ruined widows and children.
Now we snarl at the other,
blue against red, red against blue,
cocked and ready to draw,
like our opinions mean something.
If *re-ligion* means *binding together again*,
ligaments organizing the bones,
we need religion now,
binding the collective body into wholeness —
heartspeak around a fire in a sacred circle,
passing the talking stick, each to each asking:
What is it like to be you?

Ed will tell you that he attended the inauguration,
braving his way through throngs of jeering protestors.
NRA Members Only, says the sign over his carport;
Don't Tread on Me, warns the coiled rattler on his Gadsden flag.
But if you think that is all he is,
you would be wrong.
It is Ed who makes the campfire in the night
and invites all the neighbors to gather around it,
laughter mingling with crackling orange sparks in the darkness.

PREVAIL

He was a Coast Guard helicopter pilot,
a hero of unassuming honor —
rescuing frantic mariners from wild seas,
evacuating heart attacks on nights pronounced
too stormy for landing.
After retirement, he carried a broken ankle
through hip deep snow.
Semper paratus still hangs over his doorway: *Always ready.*

The first time Ed came striding up the driveway,
Wearing that tired grin under his tawny leather hat,
His calloused outstretched hand offered an unexpected gift:
Let me know when you need something.

Just after dawn on a white winter morning,
we awaken to the sound of his snow blower
roaring up our driveway, freeing us
to explore the icy mountain world.
He places his hands over ours
on the throttle of the new chain saw,
guides the placement of the wedge to avoid
the plummeting tree.

When the water filter fails and the garage begins to flood,
we know he will appear with a wrench and a bucket.
He mows a grassy path to the ancient grove he discovered,
points to the Spring's first unfolding trillium
and fresh bobcat scratches on damp ground.
He teaches us to distinguish the print of cougar
from the indented paw of a wandering dog.

The cudgel of easy judgment
drops under the benediction of his kindness.
This is how I serve my God, he quietly explains,
by doing what I can.

SYLVAN REX

Springing to life
from a damp carpet of spongy mosses
and the lacy remains of alder leaves,
this elder of the rain forest emerged from Earth
while Petrarch still wrote poetry.
With its thick, corky bark,
deeply grooved like a beloved old face,
it has reached towards the stars
and breathed the fragrant mountain air
for 650 years.
Neck muscles strain backwards to see the crown,
high as a 22-story building;
five people can barely encircle its girth,
grasping each other's fingertips.

Its canopy is full of song,
winter wrens, thrush, gray and blue jays,
eating seeds right out of pendulous cones.
Crumbs falling to earth nourish
striped chipmunks and red squirrels
scrambling around the massive base,
their quick bodies alert to owls taking cover
above, in the bristling greenery.

IN THE WORDS OF KATHERINE SEE KENNEDY

The tree took root a century before Copernicus was born,
when the universe was still crystalline spheres,
Earthlings at the center.
When the fir began pushing through thin hemlocks,
competing for light,
Martin Luther nailed his protests
To the wooden church door in Wittenburg.

It was two hundred years old
and lord of the leafy forest
when Shakespeare and Galileo were born,
and the first clock with a minute hand appeared.
Three hundred when Ivan the Terrible, in blind rage,
executed his counselors in Red Square,
and the black plague snuffed out 70,000 Londoners
in a week.
Four hundred when the colonists
armed themselves against King George,
five hundred when
Thomas Edison first threw the switch
that pierced the dark night.

PREVAIL

This towering ancestor
will be found in no book, guide or database.
Perched on the edge of a knoll
descending sharply to the west,
it is supported by an ancient cedar;
they grew up almost touching,
murmuring underground to each other
through fine white threads of mycelium.
Leaning together into the winter winds
that thunder over the mountain,
their mortal presence declares:
We too, will vanish in time
But today we live.

IN THE WORDS OF KATHERINE SEE KENNEDY

AFTER READING 'EXTINCTION DIALOGUES'

Last night, lying in bed,
we heard the roar of jet engines
screaming over the roof,
howling vibrations sucking up the air.
Only it didn't stop
and we realized it was the wind
thundering down the green mountains,
grabbing trees by the throat,
and pulling them out of the earth.
Everything was flying in the night,
the frantic wind sweeping the Earth
as if to find something it had lost.
The electricity flickered
and went dark.
I tried to explain near-term extinction to you
with the wind furiously
shaking the house by its cedar shoulders
as if to awaken us from our stupor.
I tried to describe my grief
for the cascading losses of beauty.
Guilt tore at my heart
for violating trust with Earth,
our ancestors and the children,
for having said yes to the wrong things.
You grew alarmed at my desperation
and I turned away,
thinking you did not understand.
We slept, barely, in separate beds.

PREVAIL

This morning we walked silently
through the woods.
The tooth-leaved alder
lying in our path
had assumed its future before it fell;
woody catkins are still hanging,
tiny ornaments on branches that will
never again reach to the sky.

Two gangly cottonwoods went down together.
Now their smooth green bodies lie side by side,
branches entangled.
A hemlock blocking the path at an oblique angle
cracked from the bottom,
although the fresh wood
in the damp shards of stump
looks healthy,
and the copper sheen of its skin
still reflects light.
What was it
that chose these particular beings to fall in the night,
when the rest of the forest
bent, and swayed, and stood?

Eric Dieterle

Eric lives in Port Angeles, but grew up on the sage-steppe of eastern Washington before moving to Utah, Iowa, California, Nevada, and Arizona on his journey to the west side of the Cascades. From the time he began writing for a local newspaper at age sixteen, he has known his calling and wondered if he could live up to it.

Near the end of a career anchored in words, he celebrated his memoir being published by a university press. *Where The Wind Dreams of Staying: Searching for Purpose and Place in the West* is available through Amazon.

But he's still wondering.

Contact Eric at edieterle@gmail.com

SOLITUDE, INTERRUPTED

Alone, and that is the way I like it. A five-minute drive and a ten-minute walk to deliver myself here. No one on the trail, left or right. Tree-shrouded, undergrowth-blanketed bluff behind me; gray, dimpled strait in front. A small sailboat anchored two hundred yards away, sails stowed, deck silent, reflects my attitude.

But I am not alone. Not in that way. Not in the "I can carry on a loud conversation with myself, sing (unlikely), cry (even more unlikely), take off my clothes (tempting)" way. Too much risk of being seen or heard. This is alone, not isolated. Tenuous and transient as a fallen leaf. One step away east or west by a walker or runner from being not alone. One heartbeat from the gaze of a speeding bicyclist. Perhaps already under the eye of someone unseen, looking back at me.

I turn to look east. He does not see me, but he knows I am here. Not in this very spot but here generally, connected by hazy sky and gray water, the geography of his life and my lifetime of longing. After decades of avoidance this is as close as I dare come. He knows that, too, and I count on his stubborn pride to keep him over there; he will never take the first step and knowing this I can sleep at night.

Not alone. I kept my distance and that has been enough to prevent these two manifestations—the shell containing his angry delusions and the shell containing my lost dreams—from colliding, from initiating the physics of annihilation. Not alone, and not just because I know he is out there.

He is in here, shambling through my memories, appearing unwanted in my dreams, leering with the knowledge of me he has by simply being him.

Fifty years ago, he might have died. Plenty of others did. Their bodies burned or heat seared their lungs; starved of oxygen, some traveled from sleep to death. Or awake, others jumped to meet finality in the agnostic arms of gravity. But he did not. He clamored and he clung. He resisted the easiest path to peace he had ever been offered. He lived. And obliterated the easiest path to peace I may ever know.

For two hours the morning after the fire, I knew the place he lived in had burned hot as Hell, but I didn't know his fate. I imagined it, lifted by morbid hope. Then the smoke cleared.

His time will come, as it must to all of us. My ego clings to the promise of chronology, assuming his time will come before mine. So that I can finally know the meaning of me without him.

Alone.

The sailboat has drifted, anchor line slack. A homeless man approaches. I look at him with my stay away face.

Maybe I've been here five minutes, maybe fifty years. Hard to say.

Jon Langdon

I am single and 82. I was born and raised, educated (BA in History, University of California, Berkeley, 1965) and spent four years in the U.S. Navy. Most of my life was spent in the San Francisco Bay Area, born in San Francisco and raised in Palo Alto, fourteen years in Berkeley, and about thirty years out on the Point Reyes Peninsula in Marin County, where I was a general building contractor. I have several ex-wives, two grown-up kids and two grandchildren.

I am an artist having been published in several volumes either as an artist, writer or a poet in the *West Marin Review*, and as poet in the *Point Reyes Light*. I've also been included in two anthologies of poems:, *There's A Thread You Follow* published in the Quimper UU Fellowship of Port Townsend and Volume 3 of *In The Words of Olympic Peninsula Authors.*

I now live in Port Townsend, WA where I paint and write poetry.

Contact Jon at JonathanLangdon14@yahoo.com

IN THE WORDS OF JON LANGDON

MASK

I want a mask.

Tell me, which line
shall I stand in?
First Responders,
Healthcare Workers
Cops on the beat,
Truck Drivers
who patiently stack bodies
in refrigerated trucks,
waiting,
for what,
Godot?

Has his time finally come?

Please tell me which line?

Which line will cost me
the least of my profits
and none of my principal?

Who should I supplant?
the very old,
the very young,
the very fat,
the very thin,
those I don't agree with?

PREVAIL

Which slippery slope
can I descend
and keep my moral
footing?

Please,
please tell me,
Which line
shall I stand in?

THE NATURE OF A POEM

The words of a poem
are like rain drops,
that form a pond
that is deeper than you might think.
Don't be fooled by your own reflection
or the fear of getting wet feet.
If, at first, the water seems too cold,
keep swimming
and it will warm to you.

COST EFFECTIVE

I had my cat killed
last week,
because I didn't want
to pay more
medical bills.

Like Pilate,
I washed my hands
of the responsibility
and had someone else
do the job,
but the call
was always mine.

To be kind to myself
and others,
I say
"put to sleep"
so gentile,
like a "tucking in"
with lullaby.

It was sweet,
to be sure.
We all laid hands
on him,
the vet,
her assistant,
and myself.

IN THE WORDS OF JON LANGDON

It was like
a faith healing
but a death dealing
just the same.
Resting calmly,
he didn't know that.

I looked into his eyes
until they became
that nowhere stare
that can't focus and sees nothing.

I wonder
now
about the value
of my values,
the worth of
words like trust,
care,
responsibility,
and love?

Apparently,
in his case,
for his love,
I was only willing
to pay so much
per pound.

PREVAIL

After all,
what is a ten pound cat
really worth?

If he had been
a fifty pound dog,
would I have
upped the ante
before
cashing him in?

I think
about this
a lot.
I really
really
do.

I WISH

I wish it was you
that caught the corner
of my eye
coming through the open door
not the drapes
swaying
in the summer breeze

I wish you would jump
again
upon our big bed as you retire
each night
tip toing carefully across the blanket
to gently touch your paw
to my nose
reassuring both of us
that I am still here

I see you
sneaking up
through my half closed
eyes
knowing
that you know
that I know
it's a game
that we play

PREVAIL

I wish you
could be with me
again
sunning on our porch
You
stretched out
on your side

I stretched out
in my chair
both resting
eyes closed
taking in
the healing heat

I wish
I could hear you
again
pleading
at my feet
as I mix the tuna
both knowing
I will relent
and give you a treat

I always do

I wish you could
sit with me again
sphynx like
on the shower mat
when I use the John
always amusing to me
that you would find
this a good time
to visit

I wish you
would surprise me
again
with a great leap
from the sofa
to my lap
as I watch
TV

You never stayed long
you were always stingy
with your affection
You were
after all
a cat

PREVAIL

I know these things
will pass
my memory
of you will fade
but I also know
occasionally
unannounced
when the drapes
flutter again
out of the corner
of my mind's eye
it will not be the drapes
but you
coming for a visit
looking good
dressed in your best
as handsome
as ever

IN THE WORDS OF JON LANGDON

MY BEATRICE

I'm in love with a waitress
who's younger than my daughter.

What can I say?
If Casals,
Astaire,
Henry Miller,
and Justice Douglas
can pull it off,
why can't I?

But, maybe they were
just hot water bottles
warming something
they could no longer have.

We got drunk once,
when her life was nowhere.
She was sad,
and cried on my shoulder.

Being the gentleman,
I tried to console her
with a kiss;
why not?

PREVAIL

She looked up at me,
said she saw me
as a father figure.

It's a wound
that never heals,
perhaps,
because I pick at it,
like constantly digging
in my back yard,
hoping to discover water
and the fountain of youth.

IN THE WORDS OF JON LANGDON

SOMETIMES

Sometimes, I don't want to read another's poems
and deal with *their* metaphors and similes,
or read between *their* lines,
looking for the words that are no longer there,
the shavings on the floor
of the poets' final whittled poems.

Sometimes, I don't want to smile again
at a poem of Billy Collins',
laughing and feeling lighthearted until crashing down with
the depth of his last lines.

Sometimes, I don't want to become morose again
reading a poem of John Asbury,
hating him for making me feel so stupid,
not understanding a word,
upon the first reading,
or the second
or the third.

Sometimes, I don't want to pond stroll with Mary Oliver
and muse over the beauty of an Oriole's orange breast
or the silky movement of a black snake
slithering silently through the marsh grass.
Sometimes, I just don't feel like strolling
and I hate snakes.

PREVAIL

Sometimes, I don't want to walk the hills
of some Greek isle with Jack Gilbert,
lamenting the loss of his great love, Michiko
and wondering what's left in life.

Sometimes, I don't want to read another poem
of Emily Dickinson
and wonder what kind of life she might have led
if she'd only had the services of a good therapist.

Sometimes, I don't want to read Whitman again
and feel sad and weep at a talent so great,
that the likes of it I will never have.

Sometimes, I just don't want to respond to verses
that hound me, over and over,
to be a better poet.
Sometimes, I just don't.

IN THE WORDS OF JON LANGDON

Sometimes, I just want to be sixty again
and lie with you,
snug in our bed,
spooning,
settling into the comfort and warmth of your body,
while listening to the evening rain,
gust driven to splat again and again
against the window panes,
and gaze up at our cat, Mikey,
sphinx like,
high atop the bookshelf,
peering down at us,
looking up at him,
as we drift into sleep.

Sometimes, free from the tyranny of the poetic word,
that's exactly what I want.

WHY NOT?

I think I'd like to come back
as music,
you know, God like,
omnipresent,
available to everyone as they're
able to receive,
but without rules of behavior,
the anger and vindictiveness
if I didn't always get my own way;
no requirements for sacrifice,
no sheep, no virgins, no sons,
even my own.

A lot like Kindness,
universally recognized,
universally felt,
capable of softening hearts
and changing minds.

No calls to War or violence,
in my name,
to advance some cause,
or settle some grievance.

I've never heard of anyone
going to War over Music
or Kindness.

A WINTER DAY

The rain comes,
the snow recedes.
The naive hope
the white had brought
dissolves into
melancholy puddles
on the dormant lawn.

The rain goes on,
pat, pat, pat,
a drumbeat
on the porch awning,
the tattoo of a now
ordinary grey winter day.

Linda B. Myers

Linda is a transplant from Chicago to Port Angeles with several stops in between. She slogged through a career in marketing: a few days in an ad agency will quickly teach you that fact is indeed stranger than fiction.

When Linda retired to this area, she began writing novels. She has published nine in a variety of genres, the most recent being historical fiction set on the Olympic Peninsula, entitled *Dr. Emma's Improbable Happenings*. She writes a monthly column for the *Sequim Gazette* and is a founding member of Olympic Peninsula Authors. She confesses to doing a bit of freelance editing. You can find Linda's books at Amazon and local retailers

Contact Linda at *myerslindab@gmail.com*

Author's note: In my Bear Jacobs Mystery series, Bear is a retired private investigator; his cases are documented by Lily Gilbert, and his operatives include the geriatric gang at Latin's Ranch Adult Care Home. Thanks to Joan Enoch for asking what they are up to during COVID-19. *Bear Up* is the first Bear Jacobs Mystery that is, in fact, *not* very mysterious.

BEAR UP

Case Notes
March 13, 2020

When you have a list of preexisting conditions as long as a roll of toilet paper, then wearing a mask is no big deal. That was the case for us residents at Latin's Ranch Adult Care Home when COVID-19 reared its ugly head. Among us, we have Charlie's sore nuts (from sitting on them too long in a wheelchair), Eunice's heart which clog dances instead of two-steps every now and then, Bear's ill-tempered nature even on a good day, my artificial leg and diabetes, plus a traffic jam of mobility equipment. Yet, for all our physical limitations, we stand tall on our walkers and wheels. Our busy brains have a full complement of marbles.

There'd have been little grousing about masks if Eunice didn't view anything on your kisser as an opportunity to accessorize. She'd whipped herself into a crafting frenzy, developing what she called FancyFace Facades.

"No glitter goes where my pie hole should be," growled Bear with an ursine huff of indignation.

"The feathers tickle my nose," said Charlie, who had enough issues to deal with already.

"Charms on the ear cords tangle in my hair," I explained. "I truly think the plain disposable masks will be good enough."

"FINE. JUST FINE," snapped Eunice. "But I'm wearing mine." The bedazzled hot lips on her FancyFace puckered and glittered as she spoke. I was sure her real lower lip was quivering, but of course, I couldn't see her real lower lip. Fortunately, she never pouts too long. Eunice sets disappointments aside and goes on about the business of life. "All right then," she said, brightening like a sunrise. "Maybe I'll decorate latex gloves instead."

If her paramour Frankie were still around, he would have worn any amount of decor to please "his little dove." But, alas, Frankie has crossed over to whatever awaits Mafiosos in the hereafter. Eunice misses him every day. We all do. Frankie was a dangerous man to some, but a good friend to us.

It turns out, he's still with us. This story is about the strange way the old don paid us a visit this spring and turned life at Latin's Ranch upside down.

Lily Gilbert, Flabbergasted Assistant to PI Bear Jacobs

COVID-19 made big changes in long term care facilities. Latin's Ranch was a lot smaller than a nursing home, so the rules were somewhat different but still required adjustments. All the residents wanted the place to run as smoothly as possible, knowing that Jessica, the owner, would be under increased scrutiny and stress.

Bear suggested Lily, Charlie, Eunice, and he wear masks in their living room for the first couple weeks of lockdown. "Since there are only four of us, we oughta bloody well be able to stay apart. I prefer social distancing anyway."

"Might that be because you're a retired shamus with no particular desire to save what's left of the human race?" asked Charlie.

"Fortunately for you, I'm capable of suffering knuckleheads gladly," Bear snarled although the two old men were great friends.

"I have nobody likely to visit, anyway," observed Eunice. "But Lily misses her daughter."

"It's okay, Eunice. Sylvia's so high on Cloud Nine, she might as well be in another universe," Lily answered. "When her marriage to Vinny gets past the couldn't-separate-them-with-a-pry-bar stage, maybe she'll come back to earth."

Jessica took measures against COVID-19 quickly. She asked two aides, Chrissie and Will, to stay on premise; they consented once Chrissie's mom agreed to keep their kids until long term plans were arranged. Between them, they took good care of resident needs.

The cook, Aurora, had her own family to tend, so she opted to stay away for the lockdown.

"No worries," Jessica told the residents. "I'll do the cooking myself."

When she announced that, Charlie stepped up to the plate. "I'm a pretty good cook, Jessica. Let me do that as long as the others will help."

Bear shivered. They all knew the truth about Jessica's cooking, so Lily and Eunice eagerly agreed. Bear said he'd be happy to make his Ass-Burnin' Chili as often as anyone wanted.

Jessica's husband, Ben, set up his marketing business in their apartment upstairs so he could avoid his office downtown. He took over all supply runs for the house, the pets, the horses, the rescue burros and goats. As Latin's Ranch's sole contact with the outside, he kept himself quarantined from the residents. He kept Baby Benny away, too, much to the sorrow of Bear who loved the boy to the point of baby talk. In the good old pre-COVID-19 days, "Oo woves oo, baby boo? Unkie Bear dat's huuu," could irritate anyone right out of the living room except the baby who worshipped the old crab right back. "Uka Baaaaaaaaa . . ."

The only other two-legged resident on the ranch was the barn manager, Sam Hart. He lived in an old Airstream on the property and continued to oversee all the four-leggers. Nobody else was allowed into Latin's Ranch unless an emergency popped up. No deputy sheriff, no veterinarian, no bookkeeper, no riding students, no horse boarders. The metal gate at the end of the driveway swung shut.

It was sad but bearable. The residents missed their trips to the senior center. Bear and Sam missed Reggie's Tavern. They all missed Sitting Bull, their customized, candy-apple-red golf cart. They could go one at a time, but not together. Nobody would go anyway if Eunice was driving.

Lily and Eunice took a walk on the property when the days were fine. They picked spring bouquets of addertongues and violets along the edge of the woods. They petted horse noses, the softest skin in the world, at the pasture fences. Bear, leaning heavily on his quad cane, strolled the drive to the mailbox each day. He, Sam, and Charlie continued their occasional evening chin wags, Sam inside the trailer and the residents out. Sam set a six-pack outside for them, Bear recalled old murder cases, and after a beer or two,

Charlie regaled them with lies about the women he had known.

***

In early April, Jessica answered the phone and, much to everyone's surprise, she yelled, "Charlie and Bear, it's for you. It's Aurora. She says to take the call in the kitchen."

Charlie blanched. The tough Latina cook scared the crap out of him. "She knows I've been in her kettles and cake pans! She's gonna Ginzu me like a spiral-cut ham."

"It's just a phone call, Charlie." But Bear had to admit, it was a mystery why the fiery cook would want to talk to them. Not much of one, maybe, but any mystery got his nose to sniffing the air. They took the phone to the kitchen and put it on speaker.

"Ch. . .Ch. . .Charlie here. And Bear. He's here too. Bear. Carries a stiletto inside his cane, Bear does. In case you didn't know that, Aurora."

"Hello, Aurora," Bear said.

"Hola, Señor Bear. Is my kitchen clean? Is it in order? Are you eating well?"

"Not as well as when you're here, of course, but we're getting by until you return." Bear could be a smooth talker when he chose to be, and when it was about food, he wouldn't miss a beat.

"Señor Bear, I have a message for you from Signore Frankie."

That stopped both men.

"He tells me this secret on our last Sicilian night when we cooked together in December. He knew he was not well. He made a large pot of his spaghetti sauce for Señora Eunice's birthday. It is her favorite. It is to be a surprise gift for her birthday to make her smile."

Food from her dead lover? Bear didn't know if that would make any woman smile. But he was first to admit that women were the biggest unsolved mysteries in his life.

"That's nice, Aurora. Is that all? Goodbye, then," Charlie chirped in his tenor voice.

"Señor Charlie, you slow down, and you listen. I cannot be there so you must make the meal. Her birthday is tomorrow. Remove the large pot from the freezer now. Make the spaghetti for her. Make it a party."

"Ah, sure. Party."

"You will find a note from Frankie inside the pot. I was to give it to Señor Bear on this day. I am not there. Now I count on you give it to him. Tell no one else. This is what Signore Frankie asked of us. Hasta la vista." Aurora did not hang on for closing pleasantries.

It took both Charlie and Bear to wrestle the heavy pot from the freezer onto the counter. When they removed the lid, there it was: an envelope with Bear's name in a small plastic bag atop the frozen sauce.

He opened the chilled envelope clumsily as his hands trembled . . . maybe from the cold or maybe from emotion. Bear had found the old don to be a bright spot in these last years of his life. They'd solved more mysteries, saved more lives, and prevented more crime than they had created.

The note inside the envelope felt flimsy in his oversized hands when he opened it. The handwriting was spidery and hard to read. But it was Frankie's.

Bear: Call Tony now. Grazie amico mio.

* * *

Charlie spread the word about a birthday party for Eunice, but no more than that. She was banned from the kitchen while he prepared dishes to go with the spaghetti sauce. Charlie's menu included garlic toast, antipasto, and any wine he could find, even the cooking sherry. Maybe that wasn't quite Aurora-standard, but with enough wine, they wouldn't give a damn. Lily was allowed in the kitchen long enough to make a cake for Eunice, but after she frosted it, Charlie shooed her away. He added swirls that read: *Lookin' good, babe. Considering*.

He could not help but whisper about a 'mystery afoot,' but Charlie refrained from sharing any more. "Hell, I don't know any more since you refuse to tell me," he griped at Bear.

Bear raised his eyes from the crossword. "Gonna stay that way, too," the big man said. "Unless you know a six-letter word for Monkey's Uncle, leave me alone."

Charlie's whispers were enough to raise Latin's Ranch curiosity to tsunami level, a wave of excitement crashing over them. Not even Lily could pry more out of Bear.

"What were you doing out on the patio yesterday afternoon?" she asked him the morning of Eunice's party.

"Nothing."

"I saw you frisk yourself. Either you have poison ivy, or you were looking for your phone."

"As I'm toxin-free, you may deduce that I was on the phone."

"With whom? You never talk to anyone over a minute. It took you seven. At least."

"Who are you? Mother Time?"

"Are you working on a mystery? If so, I want in. Who else will needle you into doing your job? Who else will keep the case notes? Who else will—"

"You've made your point, Lily. I'm useless without you." He rolled his eyes which, considering they were beady and dark as a grizzly, usually went unnoticed.

"If you don't tell me, I will sing *Que Sera Sera* from now until Sunday."

"All right, all right. It involves us all. I won't tell you everything because I can't break a promise I made to Frankie."

That was enough to persuade Lily to back off. Bear knew she would never want such a thing as a broken promise to happen. But when she looked crestfallen, Bear told her, "You can help organize. Be in the living room at five o'clock with your computer. Be sure Eunice and Charlie are there, too."

Lily brightened. "I can do that."

"Be sure Jessica and Ben are at the computer in their apartment upstairs."

"I can do that."

"Be sure Sam, Chrissie, and Will are at the computer in the office."

"I can do that."

"Tell each group to check email. You'll be sent a link to Zoom for a conversation."

Lily was positively cheery. "Ohhh! I've wanted to try that! What else?"

"Let me have the crossword whenever I want."

"I can't do that."

* * *

At five, Latin's Ranch thrummed with excitement. The canaries chirped merrily and even Fat Cat moved his ample self from the sofa long enough to groom top to bottom (literally). The humans were all in place at their appointed times and each group clicked onto Zoom.

The video meeting began when Tony Sapienza, Frankie's grandson and the new *famiglia* don, clicked in as the host. Everyone soon saw each other. Sam was visible in the office doorway, masked like an outlaw, six feet behind Chrissie and Will. The residents gathered around half of the game table in the living room. Lily moved the computer from person to person so they could see themselves. Jessica and Ben clicked in last, sitting together with Baby Benny on their laps.

"Baby Boo!" Bear roared in delight.

"Uka Baaaaaa!" Baby Benny roared in delight.

After that, it was decided neither of them should appear on camera. And Tony began to speak.

"First, Eunice, a very happy birthday. This call is something I would have made face-to-face if I could. But COVID-19 is not our friend. It has been nearly four months since my grandfather Frankie died. As you know, Eunice, his will was read long ago. But he wanted you all to have a birthday present on Eunice's day. And it has taken me some time to arrange everything for you. Grandfather knew he would not live long enough to see this day himself."

Eunice sniffled. But she blew her nose hard enough to jingle the bells in her earrings, and then she squared her shoulders.

"You all right, Eunice?" Lily asked.

"Yes. Please continue, Tony. I won't interrupt again."

"He told me that, while you are not *famiglia*, you are his family. So to Bear, Charlie, and Lily, along with Eunice who has already received this protection, Frankie has guaranteed you will be taken care of for all time. A trust has been set in each of your names for this purpose. It comes not only with money but with the perpetual protection of the Sapienza empire."

"Holy hell," whispered Charlie. Lily and Bear exchanged glances. They were stunned. The old don had just wiped away their biggest worry, that money would run out before they did.

"Jessica and Ben. A trust has also been set for Baby Benny, to see him through any neurodivergences that may arise from his birth mother's addictions. And to see him through college."

"Wheeeeeeeeeeeee," someone shrieked off screen. Bear assumed it was Baby Benny.

"In addition to these trusts, Frankie has a few personal gifts for you each." They all watched spellbound as Tony picked up a list. "While Aurora is not there today, Frankie leaves all his recipes and cookbooks to her. He also has provided a full course at the Seattle Culinary Academy. Frankie said he is not sure whether they will teach her or she will teach them.

"Chrissie and Will. I have selected a house for you in accordance with Frankie's guidelines. You took care of him, and he wished to take care of you, too.

"Sam, a new Airstream will be delivered for you this week, one with a floor that isn't spongy and a roof that doesn't leak. You will find inside it an antique 1894 Winchester lever-action repeating rifle, the most famous model they ever made.

Frankie believed it is time for you to retire Winnie before she explodes in your face.

"Jessica, the twenty acres of pasture adjacent to Latin's Ranch has been purchased in your name. Two fine young Paso Fino fillies will be there this week. Both are of suitable lineage for your stallion, Latin Lover. And Frankie set aside funds to expand the barn as needed.

"Charlie, a custom-built wheelchair will soon arrive. It has a motorized seat to lift and tilt to any position so that you do not have to press down on your, er, privates all day long. Oddly, it comes with an ample gift certificate to Six Waters Casino.

"Lily, an atrium will be built attached to the house, with Jessica's consent, of course. You may work with the builders and landscapers to provide the fountain, displays, and all for the flowers you wish to raise. A gardener will help you maintain it as you wish. Frankie said, 'You, Lily, will always be the finest flower in your garden.'"

The tears rolling down Lily's face weren't the only ones in the various groups on the Zoom call.

"Bear, you will never want for the finest whiskey or cigar again. And the Sapienza family will include you in every mystery that comes our way. Which are many. We honor you with our trust in your talent. And, according to Frankie, in your gentle and pleasant personality.

"Finally, Eunice, Frankie leaves an endowment to the University of Washington to support an American Crafts program, both history and application, as a part of the arts school. It is named the Eunice 'Dove' Taylor school. Happy birthday."

It had gotten noisy on Zoom as all these announcements were made. Now, everyone seemed stunned into silence.

"You should all go to the dining room now for the birthday meal prepared for you. It is a surprise as well. Celebrate and toast to Frankie, who loved you all." With that, Tony logged off and the call ended.

Charlie assembled trays for Sam, Jessica, and Ben so they could go to their own living spaces to eat. Chrissie and Will served the residents in the dining room, then left the four of them alone, along with Folly and Good Fella, the canine Hoovers who sucked up every fallen crumb.

It was a celebration but a subdued one. They told Frankie stories and drank more wine than Jessica would have allowed if she was there. But they were all exhausted. The day had been so emotional that Bear even complimented Charlie's cooking.

"Yes," said Eunice. "Delicious. As if Frankie was here with us. It tasted like he made it himself."

"Well," Charlie confessed. "He did make it himself."

"What? . . . How is that possible? . . . Is he really here? . . . a ghost perhaps?" Resident heads turned like meerkats as they questioned what had happened.

"Ah," Bear exhaled and lifted a lip in an ursine grin. A mystery after all. Together Charlie and he explained how the spaghetti sauce appeared so long after Frankie's demise. They gave Aurora the credit for keeping Frankie's secret so long.

"He thought of everything," Eunice cooed.

They scraped and stacked their plates in the kitchen for Chrissie to handle in the morning. Then each of them turned in early, Charlie and Bear to their room, and Lily and Eunice to theirs.

Frankie's room remained quiet and empty, awaiting whatever resident came next. Bear smiled a wide grin as he lumbered into his den. Oh, what hoops awaited the person who thought it would be easy to pass Jessica's standards. He or she had a helluva lot to live up to.

Case notes
March 16, 2020

Last night's birthday dinner was joyful and bittersweet, a mélange of gain and loss.

Frankie will always be with me. He has removed the terror of my final days. None of us will be kicked to the curb with no place to go. I never thought a Mafioso would be such a major part of my life. But as I've said before, life goes on in amazing ways if you just let it.

Frankie has eased our lives, giving us each things that will excite us, keep us involved, and provide freedoms we never thought we'd experience again. This all seems a fairytale ending, each of us gifted with pennies from heaven. But there is no happily-ever-after. COVID-19 may destroy us one and all, or our beloved country could collapse around us. In time, diabetes may steal my sight or my remaining leg. Charlie could drink too much at the casino and disappear into the night, a babe on his lap in his fancy new chair. Bear might be cut down by a gang of thugs on his last great case. Among us all, only Eunice is guaranteed a place with the angels.

We can't foresee the future, and so we soldier on as we are, old people surrounded by love. You know, I think I will take it back. There are happy endings at least for today.

Lily Gilbert, Loving Assistant to PI Bear Jacobs

Judith R. Duncan

I write about my chickens, dogs, friends and the beauty of the Pacific Northwest. My poems and prose are published in *Tidepools, Four Corners, Cirque, Ekphrastic,* and several local anthologies.

Contact Judy at Judy1ster@gmail.com

IN THE WORDS OF JUDITH R. DUNCAN

THE DUCKS

do not mask the virus
nor observe social distance
like the rest of us

the hen and drake
continue daily
to copulate

having duck fun
next to the pond
on my lawn

I drink morning coffee
keep my distance
admire their energy

Jeri Bidinger

Jeri Bidinger and her husband Curt open their door to the world at Spa for the Soul, an informal monastic space they created to shelter prayer, solitude, listening, rest, writing, art-making and other contemplative pursuits. They are located on a Mediterranean hillside near Kaş, Turkey. A nomad since birth, she has lived longest in Alaska and in the nations of the Middle East, where she variously practiced law, built affordable housing, taught Bible, and invited the world home. All the while, she wrote pieces of the journey, whether as legal briefs, articles, books or blog posts. She started making Turkey home in 2007. When not in Turkey, she lives in Happy Valley, in the foothills of the Olympics near Sequim, WA.

Her deepest pleasures include great books, beautiful food, outdoors in motion, on foot or bike, the creation of nurturing spaces, and living full-time with Curt. Her treasure is her kids: the natural-born, their spouses and progeny, and the surrogates. Read more about her life in Turkey in her essay "Hungry for a Mother's Love" in *The Expat Sofra: Culinary Tales of Foreign Women in Turkey,* Alfa Publishers 2019.

Contact Jeri at *jeribidinger@yahoo.com*

IN THE WORDS OF JERI BIDINGER

LAMENT FROM HAPPY VALLEY

Beyond my window, tree-edged pasture lands range into foothills. Our place lies in Happy Valley, near Sequim, Washington, east of the national historic site, land set apart to hold untouched because mastodon remains were found there.

For the last ten years we've called Turkey home, though we summer in our "other" home in Happy Valley. This year was different, though. We journeyed from Turkey to Sequim in March to attend the birth of our grand-babe. I had some business meetings in Turkey, so my husband Curt traveled ahead of me. COVID-19 erupted in Europe and US, and I barely made it as airports closed. We had tickets to return to Turkey a few weeks later. COVID-19 spread. Turkey, along with many other nations, closed their borders.

Though we didn't plan it, we left Turkey just in time. From late March, the Turkish government required everyone sixty-five and older to stay in their houses. For three long months people our age were not allowed to go for walks, or drive in their cars. No grocery shopping or going to the bank. A police permit was required to go to a doctor's appointment. "House arrest," some called it, though the intent was to protect those most at risk. In July, the curfew was modified to let old folks like us out between ten in the morning and eight at night. By fall, it was eight to five.

But we weren't in Turkey. Instead our COVID-19 journey has occurred here in Happy Valley.

I roll over to small wakefulness and crack my eyelids. What time is it? Six thirty, maybe? Dim light, still gray. I check my watch. Eight fifteen? The gray light is not dawn, but smoke. I peer through haze to barely beyond the ditch-bramble that bounds our back acre. The pastures, the hills beyond, even the sky are lost to me. When I step outside, the air feels close and smells rancid. Widespread fires rage throughout California, Oregon and eastern Washington. On the outskirts of Sequim, Washington, though, we sense no threat. The fires are terrible, but they are not here. Like with COVID-19, the smoke darkens our world and limits our living, but the flames do not touch us. Still, this morning as the world suffers, we in our Happy Valley place are touched and drawn in, made part of it, moved to compassion.

I am moved to lament.

Wikipedia describes lament: *a passionate expression of grief, often in music, poetry, or song form. The grief is most often born of regret, or mourning . . . Laments constitute some of the oldest forms of writing and examples are present across human cultures.*

Though we use the word casually, true lament is more than outpouring of sorrow. Lament, then, is an art form, a ritualized liturgy to give weight and honor to suffering, loss, injustice, terrible questions, our deepest confusion, and our helplessness in the face of it all.

It has long been my practice to come to quiet in the morning, coffee in hand. In Happy Valley my spot is an aubergine-colored easy chair close to the window. I take my journal to my side, jot thoughts and memories, events and ideas, lists — a stock-taking of the prior day and the day before me. Then I turn to the Bible. And I pray.

Through this COVID-19 summer in Happy Valley I've kept company with some of the Old Testament prophets: Isaiah, Jeremiah, Hosea, Amos, Habakkuk. These sages lived in desperate times in failed nations corrupted by wealth and power and besieged by conquerors.

As I sit in my easy chair and take in green and gold and the gradual ebb of fall that still shimmers through the smoke, how do I respond to that which besieges the wider world? To COVID-19, fires and hurricanes, and political unrest? How do I care about it? Do I care? How do I move from my safe shelter, my protected bubble of timing and fortune, to a place of compassion? So much trauma. Sickened with COVID-19, unemployed, devastated by fire or flood or wind, unable to gather in the wake of death or marriage or birth, people are afraid. Victimized by abuses of power and failures of justice, they are angry.

True lament is more than just a wail into the void. Lament is prayer, a conversation with a God who is perceived as able to prevent disaster, able to heal and restore, even able to wrest life from death; a Divine Being who engages with the world He created and loves, and who can be charged with responsibility when things go wrong. The speaker is powerless, and so she cries to a God who is not.

Lament, as an art form, bears common structure and movement. It is brutally honest, full of questions, sometimes accusatory, often angry, and vividly descriptive as it progresses from cry to calm, and then listening to peace.

First comes the heart-cry. The speaker accuses, questions, condemns, lays it all out. She may plead in humility, repentant as she owns and identifies with the wrongdoing and failure of the community. She may demand in anger, enraged by injustice and her own lack of power.

Complaint made, and rage or weeping spent, the speaker calms. Nothing has changed, but the lament moves, perhaps to memories of better times, or recalls old trauma in light of the passage of time, the coming of comfort, the growth and renewal that followed. She may waffle between past and present, but she moves towards perspective.

Laments close with a movement to hope, to peace: in a promise, in dawning change, or simply in the character of the good God. Not because anything has changed, but because the speaker has changed. This is not resignation. In the raging whirlwind she has moved into the eye of the storm, to a place of trust and rest.

Habakkuk particularly grabs me because his short book records not what he did or what he preached, but what he thought. His lament is journal rather than narrative or sermon. His place and time was Judah shortly before Jerusalem was overrun by Nebuchadnezzar's army and its population carried off in chains to Babylon. His culture and social systems tottered. Greed, lust for power, and self-protection had eroded compassion for the weak, the rule of law, and integrity in worship.

Things weren't so different in his time and place than they are here and now today. Habakkuk was angry, frustrated, and confused. He lived in a violent, destructive time.

So do I. As I spend time with these prophets I realize that I, too, have fractured into us and them, and I want God to deal with them. I've divided the world into good guys and bad guys, into my people and those others.

Dizzied in the whirlwind of our downward spiral, I've longed for, prayed for, God to intervene, to do something to correct our course, to draw people towards truth and compassion, respect and the desire to pursue goodness together. I've begged God to take out the bad guys.

But I didn't ask for COVID-19. I didn't imagine tornados, floods, or out-of-control wildfires just as Habakkuk never asked for Babylon to conquer his corrupt nation. Or political leadership that threatens insurrection in my homeland if the election doesn't go their way. All of it is so far beyond my capacity that it puts me in the way of God, and I wonder what it is all about and where it will take us. It is awful, horrible, and it is awe-inspiring.

COVID-19 is a leveler because it is everywhere. No border wall, no invasion can hold it back. To treat the world as "us" and "them" protects no one. It rivets the whole world's attention. Everyone is impacted as we shelter in place, mask, social distance, and depend on the internet for social life, physical necessities, education, health care, and the nuts and bolts of moving business forward. Not everyone is impacted equally. That is obvious. Here I am in Happy Valley

I can't see the way ahead. What I do see is an invitation.

Birds delight in the forests, pastures and ponds in Happy Valley. Here is prime habitat, and not just for geese, songbirds, woodpeckers, finches and jays. Raptors circle our sky. Not long ago fifty or so birds gathered around the feeders and waterholes off our kitchen. Overhead, two raptors made a low pass. In a flash, small bodies thudded against fence, trees, walls and windows. Panic blinded them to obstacles. We picked up five dead, not one killed by a raptor. Their fear destroyed their lives. The raptors flew on, the area too strewn with obstacles to make a dive. How often has fear driven us to destructive flight from those we name as enemy who are no real threat? Perhaps a foreigner, or a skin color, or a gender, or an idea? Dare we, dare I, allow love to replace fear?

COVID-19's invitation, the invitation of all the horrors of the time, is to stop, to stand quiet, to watch and listen. Perhaps we really do reap what we sow. COVID-19 is not a call to action. I can't run around, or pour out effort, or reason and argue, or build weapons and mobilize troops to fight it.

Because of COVID-19, families spend time together—for better or for worse. Because of COVID-19, business people and tourists no longer pack flights, fill hotels, or luxuriate aboard cruise ships. Because of COVID-19, calendars are blank, people eat in, and cars sit in the garage. So many voices that compete for our time and our allegiance have gone quiet.

No one knows what will happen, but for now we are gifted with time and one place. Along with trauma, loss, and death.

These are terrible times. But in these terrible times, air quality improves. Fossil fuels rest in storage, or remain in the ground. Tourism, profitable as it is, can ravage communities and eco-systems. For now, the earth gets a rest.

In the quiet we can, or maybe we are forced to, reevaluate our schools and universities. Medical care begins to look different. So does church, and how we vote. People plant gardens, clean and fix up homes, walk and cycle more, learn to make bread or play an instrument, and read. Sequim is seeing an influx of families who, in the slow and quiet, came to desire simpler life, smaller schools, space and fresh air. Others relocate to be closer to family, to build on relationships that matter in a life that passes by all too quickly.

Laments resolve in many ways: with a solution, a satisfying answer, a promise of future blessing.

Where will the terror and disruption of our days end? Will COVID-19 fall back under the onslaught of science and herd immunity?

I remember March, and the first shut-downs. They were for two weeks. Did we really imagine two weeks would bring the world under control? We've learned a longer view.

How long will the fires burn? How many times will we go through the alphabet to find names for tropical storms? How many more will lose jobs, businesses, family members? When we emerge from these days, what will the landscape look like? What will be the new normal? How we live will change. Will we be changed? Will I?

The worldwide trauma has hemmed us all in.

Beyond the edge of our bit of land is untended grassland. A brass plaque says that mastodon remains were discovered there, and reverences a beast long extinct. They were here. I imagine they thrived. Who knows what happened to them, but their time ended.

The mammoth reminds me that we, like the mammoth, flourish and, at some point, we will fade. In the meantime, there is a compassion that stands and watches, makes peace with suffering and change, and finds hope for all that is to come.

Gordon Anderson

Gordon has been writing poetry and prose since the 1970s. He writes all sorts of poetry: lyrics, rhyme verse, free verse, Haiku and Tanka, and Tritina, and stories. To date, he has written nine books: three volumes of *Gordito Haiku* (each having 300 Haiku and 60 Tanka poems); Chosen Poems: *Words Of Love* (a collection of 189 love poems); *Looking Through the Knothole* (100 Tritina style poems); *Morning Coffee* (126 free verse poems); *Porch Poetry* (162 rhyme and lyric poems): *Nature Poems* (105 images and reflections of nature); and *Haiku Love* (105 Haiku Love poems).

Gordon's books are available: on Amazon in paperback and Kindle E-reader.

Contact Gordon at dreamsandthoughtsga@gmail.com

IN THE WORDS OF GORDON ANDERSON

BOTH — YOU AND I

I look out my widow
I can't have my way
you're not here with me
far miles away
I work jigsaw puzzles
I try to stay sane
I wish this Coronavirus
—would just go away

I'd sure like to see you
we'd wine and dine
like in the old times
—we'd be together
and things would be fine
my dear friend— together
both—you and I

This being confined
is no kind of thrill
sometimes— I get down
and lose my self-will
I've started from seed
on my window sill
some potted flowers to grow
—I sure hope they will

PREVAIL

I think of you often
inside my heart
maybe some day
we won't be apart?

IN THE WORDS OF GORDON ANDERSON

HEADS IN THE SAND

Fishing lines an' metal cans
plastic straws an' rubber bands
cigarette butts an' paper cups
throw away stuff—just all too much

Plastic bags an' empty bottles
has got Big Blue in lots of trouble
broken glass an' rusty metal
in the sea they float an' settle

Blame it all on modern man
he don't care or understand
an' the mighty oceans an' the sands
take it on the chin—again
Now—it's pollution sink or swim
an' every day it gets more grim
—you'd think more leaders gave a damn
an' pulled their heads out of the sand

Look what we've gotten
a junkyard forgotten
with everything gone rotten

Paper waste an' plastic wraps
an' sunken freight an' garbage trash
cardboard cartons an' plywood
our human folly has mistook

PREVAIL

Will man on earth comprehend?
simply know an' understand
his human waste on sea an' land
an' have great change begin
now — it's pollution sink or swim
an' every day it gets more grim
you'd think more leaders gave a damn
an' pulled their heads out of the sand.

CONNECTIONS

I tried to call you
on my cell phone
but got no answer
so, I left a message
—then I sent
a text message by phone
which I am not good at
but maybe you'll see it
—hopefully
I wonder how you are doing?
connections
—associations, brotherhood, camaraderie
family, church, and work
connections
—and I know for sure
I'm not the only one alone
confined at home
connections
—communications, companionships, contacts
interests, hobbies, pastimes
—and I wish someone would call me
—it sure would be nice to visit a friend
—I can't wait for this COVID-19 virus to end
connections
—I mailed you a letter today
a USPS snail-mail letter
I wrote it by script
I guess I'm old fashioned

PREVAIL

I don't use Facebook or Tweet
and I only go out
when I need to
—I wear my mask and my gloves
and I keep a safe social distance
—but this sure is getting old
all this being alone with my phone
connections
—friendships, links
and relationships
with this COVID-19 virus
a real big and dangerous deal
—this distancing
and separation
so—I cannot travel
or knock on your door
and I wonder
what is the score
how are you
—are you okay?
connections.

IN THE WORDS OF GORDON ANDERSON

OKAY—I FORGOT

Okay — I forgot
I'll never forget it again
I'll never do it again
okay — thank you
it just happens
but I can't help it

So — okay — I forget
give me a break
get off my case
okay — thank you
so — I don't pay attention
I'll never do it again

Okay — I forgot
maybe I'm not interested
maybe I don't want to
maybe I don't have to
maybe I overlooked it
maybe my mind's on other things

So — okay — I forgot
maybe I can't remember
maybe I'm daydreaming
maybe I'm meditating
I'll never do it again
it just happens
so — okay — I forgot.

A PIECE OF THE PIE

Everybody wants a piece of the pie
an' so do I-I-I-I-I
everybody wants a piece of the pie

All you gotta do is open your eyes
the Population Bomb's spread far an' wide
people going here an' going there
people everywhere an' running scared

All you gotta do is see more: unfair
with added wants an' more I don't cares
with government an' justice gone astray
an everybody wanting their own way

An' everybody wants a piece of the pie
an' so do I-I-I-I-I
everybody wants a piece of the pie

All you gotta do is look more than twice
an' open your eyes great big an' wide
to see air pollution all over the place
an' junk an' ghettoes—such a disgrace

An' everybody wants a piece of the pie
an' so do I-I-I-I-I
everybody wants a piece of the pie.

IN THE WORDS OF GORDON ANDERSON

THE GATHERING

The gathering—in summertime
celebrating a July evening
at their favorite bar and bistro
which had opened once again
thirteen of them—all comrades
and of the younger generation
five ladies and eight gentlemen

Only one lady wore a mask
she sat at the end of the bar
keeping her safe distance
the other masked person
was the gentleman waiter
who worked serving them all
—from person to person he went

Three couples sat at tables
—four at one table
and two at the other
while at the bar close by
a lady flirted with two men
and two other men talked
—all of them too close together

PREVAIL

This was the engaging scene
—while background music played
a chorus of voices rang and sang
and at one time or another
all thirteen mingled and mixed
as wine and drink was had
with appetizers and tasters

When came the evening close
and it was past time for them to go
all thirteen party-going socializers
returned to their households
—twelve with contagion caught
and the pandemic raged on
—COVID-19 out of control.

Craig Andrews

I was raised in Southern California, and I loved it. In 1983 I traveled to Port Townsend to be a bartender and entertainment booker for a Sufi (yes, that's right) at Paddington's Pub. It was in Port Townsend that I met my wife. It took me less than an hour to commit to a lifelong relationship, but it took me twenty years to get used to the weather.

I have written all my life, except when I couldn't talk, but then I was thinking about it. I write stories I would like to read. And since I am a poet, I write poetic stories. I also like to steer the reader into what I call "good natured magic" and tongue in cheek impossible situations, and this for the most part, describes my life. I can hardly wait to see what is coming down the road. "Don't beam me up Scottie, at least not yet."

I have three books of poetry on Amazon. I publish poetry on Facebook but you have to "friend" me.

Contact Craig at tarasparkman@yahoo.com

FLUTE OF AMBER

A Fable For Our Times

And so it was at this time, being the year of the Dragon Moon, 1346 (for those who reckon in such ways), that there came to travel in Japan, a flutist of great renown. Verily he was well received for the laud of his excellence seemed to travel before him just as the sun arches in delight, cat like, in the pleasure of the days. All of the best monasteries vied for the honor of his sojourn, for he was a Master of the Dharma, as well as a Master of the flute.

It was said that he was born into a pious family in the land of India. While still a toddler he was orphaned by a famished tiger, but then whisked away to safety through the compassion of a Dakini, herself a disciple of the Buddha. Thus he was raised-up, and learned the music, art, and knowledge of the Supernatural Realms — the Pure Lands of Amitaba Buddha, and the Grace Lands of the Goddess Kuan Yin.

It was in the Monastery of Purple Excellence, nestled within the foothills of the Jade Mountain, that our story begins. The Flute Master, whose Dharma name was H'sien Sin (the Fairy Immortal of the Heart) had come to the Jade Mountain monastery just as the snow sealed the passes. The monastery was to be his sanctuary, his chosen place for a winter of solitude, practice, and renewal. And so it would have been except for a knock on a cold, clear January day on the monastery gates. The gate keeper was busy carving a guardian deity from Magnolia wood and just about cut his thumb off he was so startled. He never would have imagined a traveler on the road this time of the year. He rushed to open the small door to the side of the main gate, and what stood before him caused him to fart in surprise, for there, dressed in rags and standing barefoot in the snow, was the august figure of a Zen Tramp.

A Zen Tramp, it is good to remember, is a Dharma wanderer of the land. They are often endowed with miraculous powers and quick tempers. They are said to be special healers and messengers of fate, and are best left to their own devices.

The gate keeper swallowed hard. Impeccable courtesy, he realized, was probably his best defense. "Please sir," he bowed, "enter and warm yourself and enlighten me as to your needs." The Zen Tramp quickly stepped into the small room and extended his hands over the top of the charcoal brazier which was keeping everything toasty warm. He undeniably smelled of stale sweat and dirty clothes, his breath carried the odor of garlic, and his eyes had a kind of crazed look about them. The gate keeper gulped again, his Adams apple bobbing up and down like a cork midstream on a fishing line.

The Zen Tramp locked eyes with the gate keeper and held his gaze until the keeper was perfectly still. It was as if a very powerful man had placed his hands on the shoulders of a small child, calming him and holding him quiet. "Tell your abbot please," he stated, "that Diatzu san has entered his monastery, and would speak with the Flute Master H'sien Sin; and I would be grateful if you would see that a tumbler of hot sake be delivered to your gate house."

The gate keeper bowed once again. "I would be honored to deliver your message, and see to it that refreshment is brought to you immediately." He bowed again as he backed out of the inner door, shut the door behind him and let out an enormous sigh of relief as he hurried to the kitchen.

It wasn't long before the Abbot and the Flute Master entered the gate house. The Abbot, who knew of Diatzu san, both by reputation and by incidents reported to him, had advised H'sien Sin of their danger.

After much bowing, many introductions, and many apologies for such a poor and simple reception, a quiet descended upon the group. The Zen Tramp placed his foot upon the low table. The Flute Master gasped at such a breach of etiquette. The Zen Tramp dug between his big toe and his index toe and came up with a wad of mud. He rolled it into a perfect ball and holding it between his thumb and forefinger he showed it to the Flute Master. "Do you know what this is?" he inquired.

"It appears to be a small ball of mud," the Flute Master replied, "from between your toes."

"No," intoned the Zen Tramp. "It is your inflated sense of self-worth."

H'sien Sin felt the heat rise up into his head, and he was just about to reply when he felt the Abbot's hand grasp his own and give it a squeeze. He remained silent, but his eyes spoke volumes.

The Zen Tramp looked into his eyes and smiled, "The music you have mastered, and the instruments you have played, are child's play compared to the one instrument which is worthy of your lineage. Until you measure your talent and humility against The Flute of Amber, your life will be unfulfilled, and your fame will be hollow."

The Flute Master was at first taken aback, but then he rubbed his chin. "I have heard of this instrument," he mused.

"It was said in my mother's realm that back in the days before the measure of time, there was a king whose wife had died of an illness. He had a beautiful daughter who became the love of his life, indeed, to him she was life itself; yet he became so enchanted by a flute of amber that he traded his daughter to the maker of the flute. He never saw his daughter again, and he never learned more than the rudiments of music; some even said that he had a tin ear, but he always kept the flute with him. One day, while hunting in the forest, he stopped to relieve himself behind some bushes and was never seen again. The flute, of course, disappeared with him. One can only wonder at the magic which must have been crafted into the instrument. It could possibly have healed, or caused visions to appear, or taken one to different Realms."

"Those are heady things you are saying," the Zen Tramp replied. "If one is not careful they would play upon the ego until the blessing is turned into a curse. One could see that under such circumstances one would pray for the right opportunity to pass the instrument on, and what could be of equal value to such magic save the opening of the heart. I would need to remind you once again that to a master such an instrument would require the humility of a Saint."

"If I had such an instrument," H'sien Sin expounded, "I would pray every day to be worthy of it."

Diatzu san laughed. "I can see that you have a long road to travel to the wisdom of humility. However, I am but a messenger." And with this he pulled a flute from out of his robes and handed it to H'sien Sin. The room went completely silent. It was, after all, the fabled Flute of Amber. It was a rich golden brown, like the color of Fall. A small dragonfly was suspended between the blow hole and the first finger hole, captured . . . enchanted . . . destined to ride forever, the winds of song. H'sien Sin was dumbfounded. The flute felt both light and heavy at the same time. He was on the verge of fainting.

"Take the flute," the Zen Tramp said. "I will be near should it prove to be too much for you."

H'sien Sin kept staring at the instrument. Tears ran down his cheeks. The Abbot was also staring, both at the flute and at H'sien Sin. At one point he turned to say something to Diatzu san but found that he was gone.

H'sien Sin took the flute back to his cell and placed it upon an altar that he had made there for the Goddess Kuan Yin. For three days he fasted and prayed that he could be a humble servant to all that is good, and being young, he failed to recognize that what he was doing was only feeding his own sense of self-importance. He was, after all, "The Flute Master." The one in all the Realms to whom this instrument had been delivered.

On the fourth day H'sien Sin consulted the I Ching (the Chinese book of oracle). The question that he asked was, "When should I begin to play upon this flute?" He cast Hexagram #58 the Joyous. This is a very favorable Hexagram that he always associated with the Spring so he felt the message was to wait until the Robins returned with the Spring, for he also had always associated Robins with joy.

Each Hexagram, however, contains the possibilities of changing lines, and it is in the changing lines that the Hexagram can get down-home ugly and personal. He had changing lines in the first, third, fifth, and sixth. The changing line in the first talks about a self-contained joy, free from outside influence, and so, free from egoistic likes and dislikes. This would have been the mature joy so called for with the responsibility of owning such an instrument, but H'sien Sin's mind was already dancing in the possibilities of fame, and the power to "do good." The changing line in the third talks about losing oneself in outside pleasures and indulging in outside needs which lead to bad results. The changing line in the fifth talks about dangerous elements (situations) which approach. The changing line in the sixth warns that vanity has led this person to give over completely to what seems like fate but is really folly. All of these together tell a tale of downfall and humiliation through pride, but H'sien Sin did not want to see this and so lightly brushed them off as simple precautions.

Well, Spring did come, and on one glorious morning of sunshine, blue skies, and Robin song, the Flute Master stepped out into the courtyard, amber flute in hand. He sighed and looked about him, tasting his destiny; then he raised the flute to his lips and blew a single pure tone. The sound was so beautiful that everyone within hearing stopped what they were doing and listened . . . enthralled. Then he dropped the instrument from his lips and smiled a huge smile. He walked over to the bench beneath the plum tree, and his eyes danced with possibilities. He sat down upon the bench and began to play. All business stopped at the monastery, and everyone ran to the courtyard to hear and be enchanted by the "mythical" Flute of Amber. It was said that birds sang with the music that day. One even perched on the end of the flute. It was also said that there were healings and even visions of the Pure Land, the Dakini Realm of H'sien Sin's mother. One thing was certain, that a step had been taken into a prodigious fate indeed.

For two very special years the Flute Master traveled the length and breadth of the island spreading wonder, healing, and joy wherever he went. And so it continued until the day that he decided to begin his long journey homeward, back to his mother's land. If he had stayed fixed in this resolve, he could have been saved. His sense of self-worth, however, sent him to solve a problem he believed he alone could solve. Alas, he had set his destiny in perfect timing with the last changing line of his Hexagram, and it is The Way of Life that the Universe always seems to have a use for those who have lost control of their own destiny.

There lived at this time, a Warlord of great power. He lived in a grand castle in the Far Northern Realms, and he was also a legend in his own right.

It was said that he had a wife of wondrous beauty who he loved more than all the things of the Earth. She died giving birth to his daughter, his only child, and when she died, all of his joy died with her. He became dour, never laughing, never playing with his child. All entertainment ceased within his castle, and he became unnecessarily cruel, even shooting birds for daring to sing where he could hear them or killing butterflies for being too beautiful.

On the day that the Flute Master began his preparations to return home, he happened to speak with a rug merchant who had just returned from this very kingdom. He told H'sien Sin about the suffering and sadness which abounded there because of the broken heart of their Lord.

One week after this fateful day, the daughter of this very same Lord entered the gates of the monastery. She inquired about the Flute Master and the bewildered monk replied, "But surely you could have only missed him in the dark for he has gone forth to return gladness to the lands of your birth."

On hearing this, bitter tears burned on the maiden's cheeks, for she had long known of her father's tone deafness.

Know that many prayers filled the air on that afternoon as the Flute Master was presented to the Warlord in the cool of his stately gardens.

And so, as the ruler of the kingdom contemplated a "just" punishment for the audacity of the man who stood before him, the Flute Master raised the instrument to his lips. Just at this moment however, the shadowy figure of a Zen Tramp stepped out from behind a bougainvillea bush. In one quick motion, he grabbed the instrument from the startled Flute Master's hands, and soundly broke it over his head. The Flute Master, the Warlord, all of his retainers, and all of his guards went into a state of shock.

Gradually everybody turned and looked at the Lord to see what his reaction would be. His eyes were wide with wonder, then he collapsed into his chair and began to giggle. Soon his giggle turned into a chortle, his chortle into a laugh, and his laugh into great rolling guffaws. Tears rolled down his cheeks. Snot dripped from his nose, and when he finally stopped long enough to catch his breath he realized that he had, once again, found his heart.

John Norgord

John was born in Seattle and graduated from the University of Washington as a mining and industrial engineer. He moved through careers all over the US before returning to the Pacific Northwest, retiring in Sequim, Washington.

He climbed mountain all over the USA, including the first full winter ascent of Mount Olympus. He served as the second president of the revived UW climbing club and has been an active civic volunteer in each of the several communities John called home, from New Mexico to Sequim.

John has completed two novels and is working on a third.

He enjoys bridging the transition between technical writing and descriptive creative prose. With more free time as a result of social distancing, writing fills a gap that is both satisfying and exciting.

Contact John at norgordj@olypen.com

LEARNING TO CLIMB

Why do people climb mountains? To look at the other side? To behold a world apart? Maybe to meet your real self, find what you're capable of? Or maybe merely to practice a bit of social distancing. Time in a raw and rugged vastness can teach you a lot. To get there means learning to leave your comfort zone, then find your way back again.

Riding to school with Bob and Skip one morning, Skip said, "I'm thinking about learning to mountain climb. Would either of you guys be interested in taking a class?"

Bob, being his usual contrary self, commented, "It sounds like a good way to kill yourself to me."

I agreed with Bob the sport was dangerous. But I piped up, "I would be."

I've always loved the mountains, wanted to be within them as well as look at them. Could I do it? Learn to climb? Was that fear I felt already, still sitting in the backseat of Skip's car.

Skip continued, "I already checked with Dave and Paul and they are both in." Three classroom sessions were held in the evening at the community college in Everett. All four of us enjoyed meeting the teachers who enthused about showing us new skills and making climbers out of us.

The first meeting was a sort of an orientation presenting what we could expect to learn and included a schedule of class periods and field trips. The teachers were mostly fellows in their thirties and forties and as each introduced themselves, they summarized the experience they had accumulated in the climbing world. Most of them had climbed all the volcanoes in the state, and about half of them comprised the only mountain rescue unit in the west side of the Cascades for the northern area from Everett to the Canadian border.

They discussed everything from pitons and carabiners, ropes, boots and rock shoes, helmets, slings, and cold weather gear, noting some of the different features and application circumstances, to cautions on the uses of each. Then they covered making your climbing experiences safe using ropes and how ropes were handled and taken care of. After that they surprised us with our first fieldtrip to practice techniques and moves.

"Sounds like a dance contest," I mumbled early Saturday morning when we gathered at a West Seattle park where a climbing rock called Schurman Rock gave would-be climbers a chance to try out different climbing moves. We hooked up in two-man teams managing ropes and foot holds on the bunny slope of mountain climbing. All of us made foolish errors, but none of us died.

The drill established a language that a climbing pair should always use to avoid any misunderstanding. One was the climber, and the other the belayer who held the rope, sitting or braced, attached to something stable.

"On belay?" the one to climb yelped.

"On belay!" answered the other.

"Climbing?" confirmed the climber.

"Climbing," the belayer answered if he was ready for the climber to begin. Two other words often used were "Slack," meaning you're holding the rope too tight, and "Up Rope," meaning the rope was too loose and a fall could be a killer. At a point, the two team members switched positions.

We also practiced a repel, a maneuver you use to get down from something after you've climbed it. It's done by attaching a doubled over rope around a post or tree or through a fixed carabiner in such a way that you can slide down the doubled over rope. To recover the rope, you pulled one end down, the rope slipping through or around the anchor. Practicing this maneuver on a slope you could walk down was tough enough . . . much less down a vertical cliff.

Schurman Rock was riddled with cracks, knobs, bulges, shelves, slick slopes, opposing faces, short overhangs, and miscellaneous rock surface conditions. We learned to wedge our hands in cracks, laybacks holding a crack to take steps up an opposing vertical face, how to grab knobs and small cracks to pull up, and several body positions to raise yourself up the route, using only one limb at a time leaving the other three secured to the rock.

I was tired and had been scared more than once during the day. Not afraid so much as worried I wouldn't conquer my fear. We all have comfort zones – and I was pulling, grabbing, and stretching outside of mine all the while tied to another human.

Two weeks later, a large group of us headed out to practice real rock climbing on a real cliff. Outside Anacortes we snaked up a gravel road to the 1400-foot high peak of Mount Erie on its east side to a parking lot. From there we could see the roads to the west below leading to the island and an ocean channel that separated Whidbey from the mainland. The parking area was about fifty yards from the top of the cliff which was a hundred feet high with a sloped bank of loose rocks below it leading down the long chain of remaining stacked boulders almost to the water.

There were several relatively flat spots along the base of the cliff where you could land when you climbed down. We got a good three hours of repelling then climbing and were all successful at becoming familiar with the techniques and safety measures. I ached everywhere.

When we got home, I was ready for a shower. Taking off my clothes, I found a little four-legged black bug shaped like a frying pan with stubby handles crawling on my waist. Inspection confirmed I had attracted a wood tick. Sorting through my clothes, I found a second one. I called the buddies that had been with me and Paul said he had found two as well. One had already got into his skin around his waist. He described having to take a hot stub of a match to get it to back out. Skip hadn't picked up any. It's amazing how many sorts of challenges you find in the sport.

Our last field trip took us to the alpine meadow country just west of Mount Baker. A large parking area butts against the base of the mountain. We took a trail that leads to the edge of the Coleman Glacier. We had been told to bring ice climbing tools consisting of crampons, an ice ax and a set of home-made quarter inch diameter eight-foot long rescue slings for climbing out of a crevasse by shinnying up the climbing rope.

We marched out to the edge of a deep crevasse to be lowered down into the yawning chasm with our two small ropes, ready to slide one small rope length at a time back out. When my turn came, my belayer Dan set up, and I jumped over the edge.

For a slow-motion-but-split-second, I was in free fall before the rope tightened. I'd sunk far deeper than the others and my climb out was exhausting. Finally, I broke over the edge, gasping. My belayer said, "You didn't declare 'climbing' to start and I wasn't ready yet. Fortunately, I grabbed the rope and got you stopped."

Oops! I've never forgotten that correct command sequence again in my twenty-five years of climbing.

A few weeks after our training was complete, my buddies and I decided to try out our new skills. We had seen a small set of pinnacles from the highway near the little city of Peshastin on our Chelan trips. It may have been winning ugly, but we managed Trigger Finger, a pinnacle about fifty feet in circumference at its bottom, pointing up vertically thirty-five feet with a slight cock in it, coming to a four-foot around sharp point at its pinnacled top.

Years have passed since then. I've climbed everything in the state taller than an ant hill and met many out-of-state challenges, as well. Tough peaks reached through virgin wilderness and sloping hills choked by meadow grasses. Punishing climbs of great rock walls and glacial ice, with overnights in perilous positions and icy rain.

Learning to climb teaches you a lot about prevailing when the trail ahead looks impossible to tackle. Maybe you won't make it. But if you want that view of the other side and the best view of yourself, you keep going, day after day.

Lauralee DeLuca

Life is one big adventure for me. When I started crawling, I moved all the stuff from a cabinet and hid there until my parents were freaking out. And ever since, I have found a way to create adventure in my day. I enjoy retelling my tales without fabrication as my skewed view of the world leads me to plenty of non-fiction material to share.

Most of my stories come from the thirty-two years I lived in rural Alaska. I loved living far from civilization and depending on my dogs to get me around. Not all my stories are my own doing, sometimes events unfold that I did nothing to cause, like the one that follows.

Now my adventures involve living in a suburban neighborhood with an awesome view of the Olympic Mountains, getting two kids through their AA degrees, being a fiber artist, and walking the spunky chihuahua.

Contact Lauralee at arctic.spinner@yahoo.com

CURRENT STATE OF AFFAIRS

Toilet paper rationing was on. The greedy ones who had bought so much at the beginning of the crisis were forbidden to overcharge if they resold, or they would face severe fines. Though who would know? The stores limited people to two rolls per person per week. People lied so much that the stores required proof for all the people they claimed lived under one roof. The people that hadn't stocked up were rationing the amount they used at home and thinking of alternatives.

Public restrooms had to install vending machines that would dispense ten sheets of toilet paper per quarter. The desperate would sometimes empty out the machines. The few brave store clerks still working, wearing gloves and masks, had learned early not to exchange dollars for quarters for anyone. Banks had to stop selling rolls of quarters, using the excuse that they couldn't send them through the drive-thru lanes.

Since the virus had taken hold and many businesses were closed for the quarantine, the mills were not making toilet paper anymore. The truckers had been laid off, although who knows why since it is a solitary business anyway, so what was left at the mills was stuck there.

Soon the rationing was down to one roll per household per week. People were freaking out. The creative were coming up with homemade solutions left and right. One could find these on Facebook, Pinterest and other social media sites. Children and those who didn't know better would try to flush these down the toilet. Soon there were sanitation problems. Plumbers, in low numbers to begin, were in high demand and raised their prices tenfold. Many of them didn't want to take their chances getting infected so they stayed home as was prudent in these times. The poor tried to fix the problems themselves. It was a mess, literally.

The store selling the bidets was enormously popular suddenly. They ran out of stock within a week. Others were put on a list but who knows when things would be normal again. Besides, there was no one working to install them right now. Those who had them already were lucky.

The people who had GI issues suffered the most. The worst cases got written prescriptions from their doctors to allow them to get more toilet paper than the others. That caused commotions in the stores. Explaining why they could buy more was embarrassing, so they would go very early to avoid the crowds.

A few times there were riots over the toilet paper shortage. Mostly online protests, but once, over fifty people gathered, more than the state-mandated gathering number, in full hazmat suits with signs blaming the government for the shortages and demanding all elected officials hand over their supply. Everyone assumed they had access to surplus that wasn't available to the public. The media frenzy ate it up. The online sites and television stations did story after story on toilet paper: its origins, history, usage, statistics, types, brands, movie star usage, theories about the government creating shortages, fear mongering on both sides of the political spectrum. It was one thing the people could agree on, we all need toilet paper!

The virus that started the shortage soon took a back seat to the toilet paper blitz in the news. People started posting online the positive aspects about toilet paper and life in general. Conversely, people posted horrible things denigrating anything and anyone they could while lashing out over this toilet paper crisis. Several religious and political leaders were interviewed, online of course, on their feelings about this issue. Their responses were as wild and varied as the general public. It soothed no one. B-grade movie stars saw this as a chance to get their faces out to the public and made outrageous claims about toilet paper usage, history or hoarding. No respectable star would be interviewed for this scandal.

One day the news wasn't centered about toilet paper; it was back on the virus that had caused all the fuss in the first place. Apparently, while the public was so focused on a simple roll of toilet paper as well as staying home and away from others, the virus had run its course. No new cases were being found. The death toll was not near as severe as anticipated, and those who were recovering claimed the whole episode was not as bad as they thought it would be.

The governor permitted people to return to work in five days. The mills would be up and running, the truckers could bring what stock of toilet paper was still left at the mills to the stores (though it must be noted that the mill workers had plenty of toilet paper throughout this ordeal, one of the few benefits of the job). The shortage would be over soon. People didn't have to worry any more about the rationing.

Until the next crisis hit.

Steven Valadez

I have lived on the Olympic Peninsula my whole life. I have been an avid reader of poetry since I was in high school and am now thirty one years old. In the past two years I have written over seven hundred poems.

My main poetic influences are Paul Celan, Rainer Maria Rilke, Arthur Rimbaud, and Charles Baudelaire.

Contact Steven at steve.valadez@hotmail.com

IN THE WORDS OF STEVEN VALADEZ

IF IT'S ALL IN MY MIND

If it's all in my mind then I'm just going
to jump out of my skin for a minute and
clone myself a trillion times over before
I resurrect the true world into itself and then
delete the virtual black horses of the apocalypse

ALL OF THE FRAIL AND WRETCHED ONES

All of the frail and wretched ones
outside of the vortex are about to
reverse the nature of their existences
and become one with the stars and the
Angels that are about to incinerate the virus

NOW THAT I FOUND SOMETHING REAL

Now that I found something real in
this world for myself and the snarling
demon dogs of the night have been banished
away into the outer blacknesses of neverland,
I can finally grab truth by the throat and take it
to the edges of all tomorrows where I and all in all
will always exist forever and ever

Jon Eekhoff

Jon was a high school AP English teacher and an emerging author of rich talent until a fall from a twenty-foot height. Following a craniectomy to save his life, Jon's attacking his Traumatic Brain Injury with the gusto he always applied to life. He is an athlete determined to win the big game.

Jon published *A Work in Progress: Short Stories & Poems & Memoir* last year and his future goals include publishing three of his novels.

He adds, "I used to write an hour every morning . . . but I fell twenty feet and hit my head. I'm lucky to be alive. And once John Denver gave me $5.00."

His website southofthestrait.com hosts his blog.

THE COLLECTOR

I didn't really do anything. When you think about it, none of us can really make anyone do anything. We can persuade, threaten, manipulate, but in the end, most of us aren't strong enough to physically force somebody twenty years younger than us to do something they don't want to do.

I'm getting a little ahead of myself, but I wanted to get that out there before I explained, because once you find out you'll probably be like everyone else, you'll think I'm a horrible person … I'm not.

I'm a discophile, which means I collect albums, some people call them records, but that can be confusing because records can mean so many things. Like most discophiles I have a particular genre and time period that draws most of my interest: 1980s Reggae and Calypso.

I bought my first reggae albums at Tower Records in Seattle, the one on the avenue right near UW. They had a small reggae section, about two rows; almost all of it was Bob Marley and the Wailers. I looked through the albums and picked two by looking at the song titles. Two were all I could afford at the time: *Mystic Man* by Peter Tosh and *Uprising* by Bob Marley and the Wailers.

I played those records to death. I'd lie on the floor of my dorm room, plug in my headphones and listen. I can still list the songs in order on both those albums. Even today if I hear any of those songs, I'm right back there on that dirty carpet with the world figured out. They still put lyrics on the album sleeve in those days, so you could read the words while listening, or you could look at the album art because most albums were cool. Once they went to tapes and then CDs the artwork pretty much went away. Things were easier then, but I didn't know it at the time.

All my extra money went to buying albums, and pretty soon I had a solid collection. I never gave up on vinyl. Other people bought tapes and then CDs, but I kept with the records. There was something about the size, the weight, putting it on the turnstile, dusting it off, putting the needle down, and then having to turn it over when it was done. It was like you were involved in the music. Today, kids just push a button and then the music goes on and on; it wasn't like that when I was their age.

Anyway, that's how it started.

Life ended up being more complicated than I thought. It always looks like a straight line when you're young; it's not. Thirty years later I was divorced, underemployed, and looking for a way to make ends meet. When I fell behind on some bills, and it looked like I might not make my next house payment, I put an ad on Craigslist for a roommate:

"Looking for a clean roommate to share costs. Three-bedroom, two-bathroom house, rent $500. Split other costs 70/30. I'm a music lover, college graduate, and liberal. I don't watch TV. No pets."

At first, I got a few cranks looking to trade costs for yard work, or drugs, but then Ray sent me an email. I gave him my address, and when he showed up, we hit it off. He was twenty-five years younger than I was, but we shared interests and things seemed to fit.

He moved in. He only needed two trips with his white Datsun pick-up to move all his stuff. The first trip included his big things: a bed, a La-Z-Boy recliner, a couple lamps, an old dresser, and a coffee table. I offered to help him, but he was younger and managed to get everything in without any help. Then came the second trip.

I propped the front door open for him again, and the first thing he brought in was a green-lidded Bang & Olufsen BeoGram 7000 turntable. Then it was a pair of Boston Acoustics A400 speakers, you know, the type of speakers you set in the corners of your room if you want to shake the dust off the shelves, the kind everyone wanted in the late 80s, but no one could afford. When he started carrying in milk crates filled with vinyl, I decided I would help him. I went out to his truck and saw three-dozen full milk crates stacked in the back of his tiny truck bed. I knew right away that he wasn't an ordinary collector because all of the albums were in plastic sleeves. My ex-wife made fun of how I kept my vinyl in sleeves; it's the only way to keep the album art clean. It ended up being the main thing that drove us apart, I know that sounds funny, but it's true.

I picked up the first crate and tried to see if I recognized any of the albums, but they were packed pretty tight in the crates, and since they were in sleeves, I couldn't read anything through the plastic.

When I carried in the last crate, I thought I had earned the answer to the question I had rolling around in my head for thirty minutes. "Where'd you get all these albums?"

"I inherited most of them. My dad worked in the music business," was all Ray said.

"Wow, that's quite a collection. I collect too. I'd love to compare vinyl someday."

"That'd be fun," he said.

This is the moment I noticed something about Ray. I don't know how I notice these things, but I feel like I'm really good at noticing things about people. For example, I can see someone walking down the road, and from a long distance I can tell a lot about them. Predator is a word I don't like to use, because these days it sounds perverted, but it is the best word to describe what I'm talking about. I notice things, weaknesses, and I noticed Ray had this weakness, like a sadness. Nobody else would notice it, but I did. It was in his eyes.

"Well, I'll let you set up your room." I left him alone and went out to my den and picked out an album to play: *The Harder They Come*. Some people would say, Jimmy Cliff's *The Harder They Come*, but it's a soundtrack for the movie so it really isn't a Jimmy Cliff album. Record stores still put the album in the Jimmy Cliff section, but I don't think that's where it should be. I turned the volume up so Ray would hear it in his room and then reclined on my couch. It's a classic reggae album, great collection of rocksteady, roots, and ska, and it is one of those albums that most people have heard. To be perfectly honest, I picked it so Ray would come out of his room and ask me about it.

It worked.

He opened his door, and walked out into the den, "Great album."

"One of the best."

"Are you into reggae?"

"Oh yeah, it's my favorite."

"Me too. I guess I met Jimmy Cliff when I was young."

"What?" I sat up.

"Yeah, my dad worked for Chris Blackwell."

"Your dad worked for Island Records?"

"Yeah, we used to vacation in Jamaica at Blackwell's place. I think that's where I met Jimmy. I have a picture of it somewhere."

"Wait, you met Jimmy Cliff and stayed at Goldeneye?"

"You know Goldeneye?"

"Ian Fleming's place that Bob Marley bought and then sold to Chris Blackwell? That Goldeneye? Ah … yeah … I've heard of it. You've been there?"

"When I was young. Lots of times." He said it like he'd been waiting his whole life to know how special it was; I knew, man did I know.

Ray was a private guy. For the first few days he didn't come out of his room much other than to go to work and to eat. There wasn't a lock on his door, so, yes, I did go in there when he went off to work. You might not like that I went into his room when he wasn't there, but technically it was my house and I have an obligation to make sure he wasn't doing something illegal that would get me in trouble.

The first time I went in was really just to check out his vinyl. I didn't touch anything else, I really didn't.

He had all of his music arranged by the artist's last name, that's how most people do it because that's how it's done in record stores. I started with the A and by the time I got to Z I was certain that Ray's collection was the best I had ever seen.

You know that part of Indiana Jones when they locate where the Arc of the Covenant is? That is what it was like for me. Ray had everything. Sure, there were some duds, but nobody has a perfect collection, we all make mistakes and sometimes we end up with an embarrassing album or two. I mean, I remember telling my friend that The Fine Young

Cannibals' album *The Raw and the Cooked* was the greatest album ever released. It wasn't, but it's still in my collection.

Even Ray's mistakes were tastefully odd. Who still owns The Mighty Sparrow's *A Touch of Class*? Ray did. The cover has The Mighty Sparrow wearing a white tux, he's got a cane in his right hand, and the album title is in that Miami Vice day-glow pink color. Classic. There were lots of great albums released in 1985, but there isn't another album that is more 1985 than *A Touch of Class*. Songs like *Coke Is Not It, Ah Afraid of D Aids*, and *Invade South Africa* are 1985 in a nutshell, or should I say 1985 in vinyl.

The rare vinyl he had…priceless is one way to put it, but every album has a price, so I can't say priceless…so valuable is what I'll say.

He had the promotional release of *Rastaman Vibration*; nobody has that. It's the one with a hemp cover. It only went out to radio stations and media; it never got released to the public. Ray had it.

Then there was the 1973 pressing of Bob Marley's *Catch a Fire*, the one that looks like a Zippo lighter. It is the coolest album cover ever made. It had a little rivet in the cover that allowed you to open the album cover like a real lighter. Flip open the top, pull out the vinyl, and plop it down on the turntable. It was brilliant, but almost all of them had disappeared because once the rivet and cardboard wore out it kinda fell apart. Nobody had the 1973 *Catch a Fire* anymore. Ray had two, in perfect shape, like it was 1973 and not 2013.

I spent two hours looking through his vinyl, and I didn't intend on looking at anything else, but sometimes things catch your eye.

Let's say you go to a party, and you go to the bathroom. You do your business, and then you're washing your hands, and you see a bunch of prescription bottles next to the sink, just out in the open. If it were one or two of those orange bottles with the white screw tops, you might not look at them, but if there were ten or fifteen of them, you'd look. Don't act like you wouldn't because I know you would.

Next to Ray's bed there were about seven of those orange prescription bottles. Yah, I looked at them. He left them out there in the open.

There was a little of everything, sleep meds, three different opioids and a bunch of anti-depressants. It was an impressive collection, not as impressive as his vinyl.

I'm not judging, I'm just telling you what they were so you don't think the wrong thing.

The bottles were from different doctors and different pharmacies, so it wasn't like Ray was doing it the right way. On one prescription his name was Ray Griffith, on another one it was Raymond Griffith, and then there were a few with R. B. Griffith; that stuff doesn't happen by accident.

I left everything just like it was when I went in there. I didn't take any of his music, I didn't play any of it; I just left.

Remember when I said I notice people's weaknesses? Well, everything in that room confirmed what I already thought about Ray. He was weak in a really unhealthy way. I want that to be clear before I say anything else, because sometimes people feel sorry for a guy like Ray.

The next part is hard to explain but maybe if I use a metaphor or simile it will help. You know those arcade games where there's like three platforms covered in coins, and you drop a quarter through this slot to land on the platform, and it should push the other coins off? It always looks like most of the coins are ready to fall, but getting them to drop is harder than it looks. That's what I thought Ray was like. He looked like one of those coin platforms, all I had to do was to drop a quarter in the right spot and everything would cascade.

I started dropping coins.

I thought it would be easy. It wasn't. Ray was more resilient than I thought. It's funny; nobody really knows what's going on inside somebody's head. We all think we know, but nobody really does.

My ex-wife would psychoanalyze me all the time. She'd tell me I was depressed, or I needed to take more walks, or say I needed to spend more time mowing the yard…basically nagging but with a hint of superiority, like she had me figured out and knew the cure to what ails me. There was no cure because there was nothing wrong with me, nothing that getting rid of her didn't solve.

I began spending more time with Ray. We'd listen to music, talk, and sometimes smoke some pot, but neither of us partied much. We liked to mellow out and just be quiet and enjoy the common experience of listening. Music used to be one of those things we all shared. We all listened to *Night Fever* when it came out, or if you were really cool you listened to the Sex Pistols or The Clash. MTV still played music videos, and there was a common language all of us knew. These days it isn't like that. Technology changed all that. Now it's so impersonal, go online, click a couple buttons, and there it is. It feels unnatural because it is. Music has always been something humans have done together; it's part of what separates us from the animals.

I'm getting off track... Ray and I agreed about music and that built a little bridge between our worlds. Friendship is one way of putting it, but there are a few types of friendships, and this is where Ray and I saw the world differently. He trusted me; I don't trust anyone.

"After my divorce I thought about killing myself." That's how I started it. Ray asked the regular questions: How serious was I? How was I going to do it? How close did I get?

"How close? I'll show you how close. Follow me. I took Ray out to the garage and showed him the rope, showed him how I looped it over the crossbeam, and even showed him the plastic milk crate I stood on to get the rope around my neck.

"I've been there too," he said.

My heart did a little jump. "Really?"

"Yeah, I get blue and have had a few really dark times when things have spiraled into a spot that I didn't feel like I could escape."

"Hanging?"

"Huh?" Ray was confused.

"Did you think about hanging yourself?"

"Oh, I've had a couple close calls...pills twice. I thought about hanging, but I didn't want my mom and dad to find me like that."

I put my arm around him, "That's where we're different, Ray. I wanted my wife to find me."

For two months, I was happy. Ray and I started to do things. We hung out at home, we had dinners together, and we spent hours combing through the stacks at Everyday Music—one of those retro-music stores where they sell used CDs and vinyl. You'll never find a hidden gem there, it's just a place to go to look at music and remember where you were when that album came out. I'm not talking about the kind of thing that everyone experiences, like when *Thriller* was released and MTV played the video at the top of every hour, but I'm talking about the smaller connections that are personal. For instance, I can't hear *Synchronicity* without thinking about working in this kitchen in Bakersfield between my senior year and college, or if I hear Teenage Fanclub's *Bandwagonesque* I think about meeting my ex-wife…that kind of time traveling is what I was saying.

Ray had a few of those albums. Radiohead's *The Bends* was his senior year in high school, and he was working for a lawn care business: he said he couldn't hear those songs without smelling fresh cut grass, and then there was *Evil Empire* by Rage Against the Machine. Ray made a mistake by telling me that was the album he listened to when he was in his darkest places; the first couple times he tried to kill himself.

I bought a copy of *Evil Empire*. You probably don't believe that music leaves marks on places, but I do. I mean the actual sonic waves stay in the air even after the sound is gone. Like, if I play *Synchronicity* the reason that it takes me back to that place in my life is because my cells are all marked by those sonic waves. The same thing happens to places, too. If you play an album a lot it gets buried in the wood and carpet of a room, I know that sounds weird, but think about it, it's physics or science, or whatever.

So, each day, when Ray left for work, I went into his room and put *Evil Empire* on the turntable. I'd turn the volume up to the top; close the door and let Rage loose in the room. When side one was over, I'd go in and play side two. Each day I'd play the whole album three times because three is the magic number, or whatever.

A few days into my experiment Ray started dragging around the house. He had that hang dog expression and body language people get when they're spiraling down into the darkness.

A week into it Ray was openly talking about not being able to sleep and how he was feeling depressed. I asked if he was taking his meds; he said he was, but they just didn't seem to be working. "Maybe you should stop taking them for a little while," I said.

I don't think you can prosecute me for that, I'm no lawyer, but telling someone to stop taking their meds, especially if they're an adult, isn't against any law. It wasn't like I walked Ray out to the garage and said, "Remember I left this rope here. If things get too difficult here's where you can end it all."

Now you know. I mean, it wasn't too long after Ray stopped taking his meds that I found him. I told him I was going out and would be back in a couple hours. When I got back, he wasn't in his room. His truck was still parked out front. I had a feeling I'd find him in the garage. I did.

I called 911. I didn't have to put on an act because I really was upset. I thought it would be easier, but I really did like him. Before the cops arrived, I went into his room and got the rare vinyl. I'm pretty sure he'd want me to have them.

I slipped them into my collection, and that's where they stayed. One of our favorite songs to listen to was Bob Marley's *Pass It On*. I like to think that Ray would understand.

Derek Huntington

I was born and raised on the Olympic Peninsula. I spent many summers hiking mountain and beach trails while questioning life's many mysteries. Writing down my thoughts has brought me a clearer understanding of the perplexities in living. Writing is my therapy and as I grew, I came to realize that I could express myself through writing when I couldn't convey my thoughts and felling verbally.

I enjoy history, sports, and reading. Stephen King is my favorite. Family is also a component in my life. I have a wife and eight-year-old daughter.

Contact Derek at derekh_1985@hotmail.com

ESSENTIAL

Essential.
So I am called.

I'm an introvert.
An introvert with anxiety and depression.
so you'd think this coronavirus pandemic
would be hard on me,
but really it's not.
It has actually been a blessing in disguise.
Since I'm an "essential" worker
not much has changed for me,
other than my daughter not going to school,
but that doesn't really bother me that much.
It means I get to spend more time with her,
which I'll never complain about.

Since I'm an introvert,
an introvert with anxiety and depression,
an introvert who is an "essential" worker,
this pandemic has actually been good for me mentally.
It has been a blessing in disguise.
that may sound weird,
but I've actually been happier since it started.

I'm not a big people person,
so this social distancing,
and stay-at-home order is perfect for me.

It's a blessing in disguise.
If I don't want to be around people,
I don't have to be,
and now it won't be considered rude,
because I'm just following
the recommendations put in place,
to help stop the spread.

Essential.
So I am called.
Am I okay with that?
Am I okay with being "essential"?
Yes and no.
Yes because I still have a job to go to five days a week.
I still am earning money.
Although I heard people on unemployment
are making more by not working.
So those out there risking their health,
aren't making as much as the ones not allowed
or not wanting to work.
I've been working even more
because so many people don't want to,
because so many people are choosing to self-quarantine.
I could self-quarantine for two weeks
but I don't want to waste my vacation on that.
I'd rather use it when I want.
Also because there is always a chance I could get it.
I'm being careful but maybe it doesn't matter.
A lot of people aren't following the stay-at-home order,
and since so many things are closed,
Where do people go?

Essential businesses.
It's like their new vacation spot.
And do you think they follow the social distancing?
No.
They're wearing masks and gloves
so they think they're protected,
but that's just not the case.
So now we "essential" workers are even more at risk.
It's never going to get better,
or back to normal,
if this continues.

Essential.
So I am called.
Whether I want to be or not.
Whether I'm happy about it or not.

Susan Erickson

Hi, I am Susan Erickson, and I am living my retired life in Sequim, Washington.

I spent over thirty years living and working in Alaska. I was born in Cavalier, North Dakota, which is where most of my childhood memories originate.

My journey as a writer began with a community ed class on *Writing Your Memoir*. Since that class, I contributed a number of stories to the anthology, *Seqribblers Gone Wild*, available on Amazon.

Contact Susan at sgeak61@gmail.com

MY BROTHER, BORIS BADENOV

It's no surprise. Everyone knows that it took my mom two different colleges to finally complete her M-R-S degree. And it's no surprise that she quickly followed up with the tea for two advanced degree. Yep, she was the kind of woman who, after Daddy put a ring on it of course, sang under her breath, "a boy for you and a girl for me, can't you see how happy we would be." For my mom, after all her hard work and labor, just shy of ten months after the September wedding, the first baby arrived. Only fourteen months later, baby number two showed up on their doorstep. And those babies came in the right order—boy first, girl second. And yes, she was happy.

I was girl second. I will be the first to say it: I was not happy with the situation. After all I was baby second. Who has time for baby second? Mom had lots of time when the crown prince was the only child. She had time to complete his baby book with every milestone, the family tree, locks of his first haircut. You name it. She had it carefully recorded. No doubt she recorded every burp, too! My baby book had my name recorded and one or two measly milestones. Who knows when I first crawled or burped. It was so incomplete you probably could have used a good eraser to remove all the entries and sold it for new at a garage sale.

I was okay with having a sibling. I could learn from all his mistakes. And he made many. But why couldn't he be older. Much older. So old that he would treat me as the adored baby sister—the kind everyone wanted to protect. Instead I was stuck with a brother who liked to torture me, a miniature Boris Badenov in training.

My brother probably hated me for taking away all the attention everyone paid him. He was first. He was a boy. Therefore, he was the little prince. Adored by all. Then I came along—cute as a button—and stole the stage. No one on this planet, dead or alive, will ever convince me that he was the kind of older sibling who would gently pat my cheek or willingly hand over a toy for me to play with. I did have the advantage most of the time though. Whenever I wanted something he had, I just had to turn on the crocodile tears and tell whoever was near that he hit me or he stole my toy. Pretty much worked like a charm. He got admonished, and I got the toy.

Yet as time wore on, my bother became the wiser of the two of us. There must have been an intensive program at the Boris Badenov Charter School because all of a sudden my brother began a different kind of torture. More subtle. He learned to look before acting like when he dumped a bucket of bathwater over my head the minute mom walked out of the bathroom. He would hide my toys. For some reason he always seemed to take my favorite Flintstone jelly glass for his orange juice in the morning. Perhaps the lowest, most blasphemous deed was hiding my little pillows. Or worse yet—farting on them! That was low.

When he began to realize that cutting the cheese grossed me out, he found every opportunity to torture me with the flatuous act. No matter how much I complained he kept passing gas. However, enough was enough.

What was my breaking point? The time we were in the bathtub. I was minding my own business playing with the floaty, multi-colored toys when my brother tapped me on the shoulder and pointed to his butt. He lifted one butt cheek and all of a sudden bubbles furiously began popping to the surface. An odor worse than Limburger cheese followed. I shrieked so loud Mom came running. When my brother couldn't stop laughing amidst my tears, she asked what he had done. When I told her, she tried but was not very successful at hiding her amusement.

After the bath explosion I demanded bath time without the nefarious mini Badenov. I enjoyed the alone time in the bath. I could play with any toy I wanted without having to share. Mom had no problem with separate bath times as it kept the peace. If my brother tried to interfere, Mom would close the door creating a barrier between us and him. Eventually my little brain put two and two together, concluding that distance was the key to keeping my flatulating brother at bay. Social distancing circa 1963.

Samantha Hines

Samantha Schmehl Hines was born in Spokane, and currently quarantines in an increasingly small house in Port Angeles with two kids, her cat, and occasionally her partner. A librarian and primarily a writer of boring academic publications including two dull books and a somewhat less dull doctoral dissertation (forthcoming in 2021).

This is her first published work of fiction since sixth grade. She hopes it will not be the last!

Contact Samantha at samhines@gmail.com

KEEP YOUR DISTANCE

I grew up in a family where only two emotional responses are allowed: toxic positivity (for women) and anger (for men). I've never been great at performing my gender, so for me I defaulted straight to anger. However, I have just enough of my mother in me that the anger tends to show up as righteous indignation for the underdog in whatever situation I find myself. It's not a great mix — end up fighting the power way too much to get anywhere in life.

When the Stay Home order was issued, I was between homes and between jobs, living off the last of my savings in a small town on the Pacific Northwest coast. I had plans to go up to friends in Canada but didn't move fast enough before the border closed. I had a feeling they were more relieved than upset that I couldn't make it after all. So I decided to socially distance out in the woods and hope that I wouldn't get asked to move along anytime soon. Maybe this was my chance to write the Great American Novel, I joked to myself, thinking of all the writers that were probably both delighted and terrified to have this gift of time and the societal encouragement to not waste a moment that could be devoted to capitalistic pursuits.

I drove around until dusk, stopping at a small camp store in the middle of nowhere to inquire if there might be a place where I could stay for a bit. The proprietor, perhaps thinking of the long-term absence of tourists for the season, cut me a deal and suddenly I was no longer homeless, at least for the next month. I stocked up on supplies and headed to the most remote campsite available. It looked like keeping distant from humankind would be absolutely no problem here. I set up camp and fixed a simple dinner in the dwindling daylight, then read by lantern for a couple hours until a reasonable hour for sleeping arrived.

I snapped awake in the middle of the night, uncertain what woke me. Then I realized I could hear a soft, small whimpering out in the trees, then a growl considerably closer than I'd like to my tent. The whimpering stopped.

I'd like to say I weighed my options and considered what an appropriate response would be. "I knew it had to be a wounded animal, chased by a bear or a wolf," future-me might explain at a party. "If I made a loud noise, the attacker might run away," I'd say to the person on my right. "So I figured I'd try to scare it off and see if I could help whatever was hurt," I'd declare to the room at large. But I'm not that thoughtful generally, and something happened that made my brain shut off.

"Please . . ." whispered a quiet voice in the woods. "Please."

I heard another growl. It was further away from me than it was a minute ago, but not by much. It was now closer to the quiet voice.

I was out of the tent, shouting, before my brain could engage, I had no idea what, just making as much scary noise as I could, the only thing close to a thought in my head being that I had to fix this, I had to solve it, I had to make the bad thing stop.

Luckily there seemed to be a lack of thinking going on that night in general, and whatever was growling took off like a shot when I appeared on the scene. I took a deep breath to try to keep my heart from exploding and to try to kick start my thinking process. "Hello?" I called out softly. "It's okay, I want to help."

"No! Stay away!" the voice whispered.

I reached out instinctively, like the idiot I am. When my fingertips made contact everything went cold and black. Over the sudden roaring in my ears I could hear myself pleading, "Don't leave me, don't leave me." I was twenty years old, holding my dead cat in the veterinarian's office, weeping. "Don't leave me, don't leave me." I was twenty-seven years old, begging over the phone from a nondescript hotel room somewhere in rural America. "Don't leave me, don't leave me." I was thirteen years old, watching my mother back out of the driveway. The pain and the loneliness swallowed me up, and I dropped to the ground, clutching my head.

I don't know how long I laid there, cold and stiff, the only sound my rough breathing, but then I slowly came to awareness of another sound. The growling had returned, and it was getting closer. I heard footsteps crunch on the forest floor, not a person, but a large animal of some sort. I held my breath, my mind frozen with fear.

Something snuffled warm breath over my numb feet. I was too terrified to open my eyes, too terrified to think. Whatever was sniffing me paused, holding still in the now-silent night. We both listened, but only one of us knew what we were listening for. A soft sound edged into my hearing off to the right, almost like a dream. Almost before I had heard it, whatever was looming over me was off like a shot, running into the woods toward whatever had broken the silence.

I internally counted to a hundred, then a hundred more, like I did back when I was a kid. It was magic back then, knowing that if I held still and quiet long enough the monsters would leave me alone. Tonight, I was no longer so sure. But, eventually, I had to move, just like back then. Stiffly, I made my way to my feet. I felt sore all over and cold down to my bones.

At a loss, I got in my truck and started the engine to run the heater a bit. The sound of the engine made me flinch as did the sudden flare of the headlights. I peered out into the darkness, but saw nothing out of the ordinary. Everything seemed bland and dull and usual. I started to wonder if I was going crazy. I wondered how I would know if I was crazy, out in the woods all alone. How would this story sound at a party, I wondered idly. Would there ever be parties again to tell stories at.

I decided to stay in the truck with the engine running until the sun came up. I would talk to the guy at the camp store, see if I could get a refund. Either way, I'd cut my losses and go back into civilization and find a place to hole up there. No matter how terrifying the pandemic is, how isolating, we're all going to die sometime, and there's degrees of dying alone. I'd rather die alone where things used to make some sort of sense, instead of out in the wilderness.

Dianne L. Knox

My name is Dianne Knox. Fact. I live in Sequim. Fact.

Writing is not a team sport. A writer is a quarterback throwing metaphors into the End Zone, a running back running sentences in yards of rhythm, kicking one last "point" through the goal posts. There are times you want to hand the ball to someone else who can find the right word that puts your poem in the air and scores the reader's heart.

My training in writing alone has helped me in these COVID-19 times. But, please, I am not lonely in this aloneness. Cheering crowds are in my head, though not always as loud as at the Clink. Fans make appearances as friends, family, my alter ego/love, who encourage me to practice through a slump.

I am a Seahawk season ticket holder. Fact.

Writers are often asked why they write. A better question is: Why do YOU not write poetry? Because you don't see beauty? Can't feel? Haven't touched or been overcome with sensations? You don't write because nothing is screaming inside of you, forcing you to pen it? When I don't write or read, an emptiness fills my hands. It becomes a sad day, incomplete. Then comes tomorrow.

Contact Dianne at dianneknox@icloud.com.

TRIP

I pick him up.
We drive to Silverdale.
My right hand squeezes
His left thigh.
He lifts my hand tenderly
To his mouth and places
The most exquisite kisses
On both sides.

In that moment
Out in the world
Traveling down the highway
We are closer
Than all of the intimacy
That can be squeezed
Into life.

I BOUGHT VINE TOMATOES INSTEAD

She's the COVID Queen
Number nineteen
Don't wear no mask
Don't you ever ask.

Thinks she's above what's needed
Can't mind what everyone else has heeded
Marches to her own drummer
Individualism that couldn't be dumber

Seeing her at my market, Sunny Farms,
No clue how many she harms
Squeezes every Roma tomato
Without gloves, not even for a Russet Potato

Am I being an over-reactor?
Seeing her among veggies with no protector?
Breathing onto tonight's dinner
In my eyes, she's a true sinner.

When we see a lull
In this time so awful,
If I see her face again,
I will chastise her nonchalance
Condemn her viva la difference.

IN THE WORDS OF DIANNE L. KNOX

DELIVER US

My mail lady
Just drove by
My family room window
In her white
Mail van
Blue rubber-gloved
Hands off the wheel
In the air
Waving to a beat
On her radio
Singing with a smile
Delivery, Corona Virus-style

What a joy.
I'm going to wander
Out to check
My happy mail.

SHELTER IN PLACE

Shelter in place
My space
My face
Shelter here with me

We will shelter each other
Need to shelter one another
Must shelter in safe
Shelter in place

This is my essential business
Taking my walk daily
Along Marine Drive
Under sheltering blue skies
Eagles guarding babies
From my curious eyes
Keeping social distance
Breathing fresh in my space
Seeing others from a six-foot buffer
On my pace
Touching others with my sight
Holding air in lungs clean
From COVID-19

IN THE WORDS OF DIANNE L. KNOX

Isolate after exposure
Try for composure
Trying times for sure
Shelter with me here

Make space for my face
On your shoulder
As we shelter in place.

TORRENTIAL REINS

He always told me there was nothing
More powerful than the force of water.
He didn't know his own death's impact.
Washing over me like a hundred gallons
Of drowning sadness.
Cascading torrents of memories
Pounding my senses,
Swelling the banks of my heart,
Flooding my ears with the
Depth-song of our life.
Fathoms of love,
Thousands of leagues
Under this heaving sea of tears.

IN THE WORDS OF DIANNE L. KNOX

PESTO CON COVID – EVERYONE IS COOKING

There is love in every
Press of the pestle.
Juice of the squeezed
Basil leaves,
Combined with pine nut meat
Are elevated
When pressed garlic
Kisses parmesan.

The mixture explodes
On your tongue
When we dip a chip
To savor the sides
Of the mortar,
That has blended
Our tastes
Creating an emotional pesto
That lingers
On our breath
Turning our boring spaces
To delicious adventurous places.

PREVAIL

Louise Lenahan Wallace

I always knew I wanted to write, but never believed I could do it "for real." My first novel took twenty-five years to be published. Thankfully, the next four came more rapidly.

All of my books are available on Amazon and my website: *Length of Days, Day Unto Day, Children of the Day, Longing of the Day,* and *Day Star Rising.* My sixth book is underway. In addition to receiving several writing awards, my non-fiction articles have been included in *Chicken Soup for the Single's Soul,* in Chicken Soup's *The Joy of Christmas,* in Peninsula College's *Tidepools,* and in *Grit* Magazine. My advice to beginning writers, "Don't give up your dream of writing." I received enough rejection slips to paper *two* walls before my first novel was published. But when it happened, it was exactly the right time and place.

Contact Louise at lwallace@olympus.net and louiselenahanwallace.com

THE BEAR FACTS
OF KEEPING ONE'S DISTANCE

Cra-s-sh! Bl-l-a-ng!

"Get out of here, you rotten, no-good, son of a . . ."

The bears had struck again.

During the summers of my childhood, Dad's vacation meant a family camping trip to a national park. Grand Canyon, Yosemite, Zion—each year Dad and Mom, my two older brothers and I visited a different place, but all shared one trait that, because of its recurrence, became a standing joke: Wherever we went, someone—family or stranger—was sure to tangle with a bear.

I was ten the summer we camped at Crater Lake. The ranger warned us on our arrival the park bears were acting troublesome, and crossing them was extremely dangerous. We had had enough "bear encounters" previously that we knew to heed his advice. But someone else didn't.

Day and night the shaggy creatures strolled past the campsites, their red-black eyes glittering, moist black snouts snuffling as they swung their heads from side to side, their long, sharp claws wickedly ticking off stones and pebbles in their path. They ignored the human beings who eyed them with open curiosity and, perhaps, hidden fear. Their appetites ran to more succulent game — the contents of the trash cans — and day and night they served themselves liberally. Unfortunately, someone neglected to mention to them the vast difference between garbage can snacking at one o'clock in the afternoon and at three o'clock in the morning.

Peaceful silence of nighttime drifted over the campground as yawning vacationers burrowed into beds, bunks, and bags. Stars shimmered overhead; the breeze soughed through the pines.

Br-r-a-ng! Clunk! A trash lid spun wildly into the darkness, in mid-flight smacked a neighboring can and ricocheted to the ground.

Whump! The can thudded to earth. And another four-footed thief feasted.

The bears conducted this "Garbage Can Symphony" at least a score of times during the next hours. No sooner did we settle back than the sleep-destroying refrain began again. Knowing another nerve-shattering crunch was coming, but not precisely when, added much to the thrill of the performance.

Suddenly a crash louder than any previous one sent echoes rebounding through the trees. A most horrific cacophony of growling, cursing, crashing, huffing and scuffling erupted. An outraged roar — animal or human? — brought scantily-clad campers piling out of tent doorways in time to glimpse an enormous brown bear, ears laid back, head tucked down, charging full-tilt across a nearby meadow. Full moonlight illumined the grassy expanse, etching clearly the details of hunter and prey as, fetchingly garbed in nothing but a short undershirt, an irate camper galloped close upon the hapless bear's tail.

The gentleman had, apparently, spent part of the preceding nails-screeching-on-chalkboard hours teetering on the brink of his personal fault zone. Having finally plummeted over the edge, he was going neither gently — nor quietly — into that good night. Bellowed curses and pithy observations about the bear's folks interlaced with screamed comments such as "Take *that*!" and "See how *you* like it!" as, violently whanging two metal trash can lids together, he chased the terrified animal across the meadow, into the trees. The chime of cymbal-crashing lids, echoing faintly, marked their progress long after the pair disappeared from sight.

The rest of that night, except for an occasional chuckle, silence reigned in that part of Crater Lake.

Pamela S. Kuhlmann

Words that so often escape me in conversation have always come easily through my hand. So often, a stream of words, the perfect ones, stop me in my tracks. They begin to form themselves. I must grab a pen and write them down before they are lost. They are so elusive that way. Always I have been writing. My soul is never satisfied until the feelings have expressed themselves on paper. Sticky notes of thoughts, ideas, inspirations color my world. The process never stops. I will continue to write as long as I have something to say.

I grew up in Sequim, WA, more specifically on a Rural Route in Carlsborg, long before the Mill Pond was drained and the darling General Store closed its doors. It was the scene of a bygone era, a place where a writer's mind could really play.

As a young woman, I moved to Pierce County where, while raising a family, I lived and worked until returning home a few years ago. These days I lead a weekly Meditation Group, and I travel wherever I can.

You can follow my story and my inspirations as J.S. Burgess on my website www.fromasoul.com

THE SOUND OF PEACE

I didn't start on the spiritual path intentionally. One day, I simply stopped trying to fix things. I stopped looking to others. I stopped interrogating the world. Fueled by frustration at life and the condition of things, I naively began asking questions.

"What am I really doing here?"

"Why does my heart ache with unfulfillment?"

"What does my soul need, why does it beg for so much more?"

"Why does everything I want seem so far out of reach?"

I thought I was just asking questions; I had no expectations. One day's inquiries led to the next. I was posing questions, exploring, picking up clues, and innocently following trails without any real agenda.

It was a weekday in January of 2014, the first time I sat down to meditate. I don't remember exactly what day of the week it was. In many ways, it was a day like any other, except that, if I had a choice, I would much rather have been at work.

For years, life had been very difficult. I was newly divorced. Everything was shaken up, but we were recovering, the kids and me. It seemed that details were working themselves out, and we were getting a taste of what our new lives might look like. But, just as tectonic plates must rock and shift before they settle in for a while, so it is during times of great personal transition. As such, the next quake that came was in the form of a layoff notice, just before Christmas, the latest in a long line of undesirable circumstances.

I had always been a doer, a planner, a list maker. Nothing was going to catch me off guard. Every detail was noted, thought through, factored in. So, how could this happen? The one constant, the single thing that I could always count on was that I had a job. Not only was I outraged, but I was absolutely terrified.

The last work day of 2013 was New Year's Eve. Most of the staff was home enjoying the end of the holiday season with their families. I had been selected for a layoff to help balance the budget in the new year. I was squeezing every last hour in. Late that evening, I walked out of the building and down the stairs alone, in the clear, cold, winter night. The stars were out. I had no idea what we were going to do. There was a mortgage, there was food and utilities. There were two teenagers at home. With all of this on my mind, I heard a voice come up from deep within. It said, "Keep your eyes open because you're not going to believe what happens." I didn't recognize this voice as my own. Then a thought came, "At least now I will have time to meditate."

On the first January morning that I sat down to meditate, I hadn't bothered to do any research. I didn't know what meditation meant or what I was trying to accomplish. I had only heard that it was good for me. That was all. I didn't know why. I didn't know how. I thought that people who did it were weird. How I had come to that conclusion, I wasn't sure. I didn't want to be one of the weird people who meditates, but it was a new year and I was unemployed.

I was the only one home and the house was quiet when I began. I closed my eyes and listened to the stillness with an interest I hadn't cared to engage in for a very long time. Faintly, I detected a sound in that silence, a hum. It reminded me of a sound I had heard one day as a child when I was sick in bed and home alone.

The sound I heard as a young girl was so distinct that, at the time, I wondered why I had never noticed it before. It was ceaseless and light, but almost piercingly obvious. Paradoxically, it was the first time I could recall hearing it, yet I recognized it. There was a familiarity to it. Somehow, I could feel the significance in it. Although I was a child, I could sense that there was something more to it than just a sound. It was almost calling me. There was something behind it, but I couldn't place it. I listened intently for the longest time, hoping that the answers would come, although they never did. Intuitively, I suspected that someday I would understand what seemed to be right there.

This childhood experience had been so profound and so memorable that every detail of it came back to me in an instant. It was as though the experience itself had been waiting for me to return to these very conditions. In my meditation, I decided to put all of my attention on the hum of that silence. It was the only thing to do.

Again, I noted that, primarily, I tuned out this sound; but once it was detected, there was such continuity, depth, and substance to it that it couldn't be dismissed. Why was it here? What did it mean? What was it doing? Here was the same mystery I encountered so long ago, as well as the feeling that there was a part of me who already knew and had always known what this was. As I tuned in deeper and deeper to the sound, it began to feel as if the hum and I were completely alone. There was the hum, there was my listening, but nothing more.

As I stayed with it, I began to feel a tingle in my toes. First in my right foot, then spreading to both feet. I watched and wondered while not allowing my connection with the hum to break. I followed the tingle as it gradually made its way from my feet, up my legs, into my abdomen, my upper body, through all my fingers, both arms, my face, and exited out the top of my head.

I sat in total bewilderment, stunned at what had taken place. It felt as if the hum was the sound of what was holding everything together. It has been said that everything comes into form through the vibration of sound waves. It would be years until I could understand this. But what I did know, as I explored this experience I had with sound, was there was a mysterious element of power to it that I could not ignore. There was a part of me who had been waiting for this moment and knew what to do.

There was substance, there was wisdom, there was direction in this sound I could hear in the silence. My inner self knew that. My inner self knew the way. My inner self was uninhibited, unintimidated, completely fearless. I was still unemployed. I still had no idea how we were going to come through this, but amidst all of this worry an adventure was unfolding. It was so enticing that I couldn't stay out of it.

There seemed to be things waiting for me there. Specific things, experiences, that were designed just for me. Designed to give me the answers I was looking for. Enough to offer clarity. Just enough to keep me coming back, but not so much as to be overwhelming.

I was so completely enchanted with my experience of harmonizing with this sound, that I began to experiment with it. Where was it coming from? Undoubtedly, it was from somewhere deep, deep within me. Was it still there when I closed my eyes and listened for it? Yep, every time. What was it trying to tell me? Follow me, it seemed to say. I could sit with it long enough to follow the sound back, as far back as I could go. All the way back to its origin, it seemed. If I wasn't mistaken, it was, in turn, leading me to the source of mine.

Knowing nothing about spirituality, meditation, or yoga, this sound became my mantra. I could listen to it with absolute attention and it would take me to an encounter with blissful peace. I did not know that life included moments such as this. The place it took me was everywhere, but it was nowhere that I could describe. It seemed like it was beyond the mind; it was behind the mind, and above the mind. Curiously, I could get there only through the surrender of my mind.

As time went by, I began to see the trail of my life curving behind me and in front of me as that of a hero's journey in any novel. It was a new role for me, one of hero instead of victim. I liked this heroine. We were strangers as well as old friends. I could settle in at the front row and cheer her on. Things inside of me were stirring and rising up. Forces and sources within had awakened that had never before been part of my consciousness. These were things that I didn't know. Intuition just knew what came next. Confidence told me to let go of worry, just keep coming back to this place. Trust reminded me over and over that this could be the best thing that ever happened. Meditation and tapping into this sound in the silence became part of my daily routine. I paired it with applying for every vacant job that I thought I was qualified for. Each day more of what I needed came to me in ways I could never have organized. The heroine played her part courageously. Together we watched and waited.

Things were working out. We were getting by on unemployment and food assistance. The awareness of the moment I was experiencing in meditation was spilling into my daily life. It was demonstrating how to access my inner power – (Be fully immersed in where you are, let the future take care of itself). The utter helplessness and powerlessness that I felt was giving me a sense of fulfillment, of meaning, that was stronger than the fear. It was filling in the vacancy I had always known to be part of life. This process was empowering me, whispering the possibilities; not only over the immediate circumstances, but to the overall purpose of my life.

On the sixth week of unemployment, my phone began to ring with offers for job interviews. It rang all day, for days. Once enough steam had built up behind my intentions, there was no stopping it. Job interviews had me driving through the three surrounding counties. I had so many interviews that I started declining them. I couldn't get to them all.

Then, on the seventh week, my old employer called to offer me my job back.

When I went back to work, I went back as a different person. In a job that I had always seen as nothing more than a means to an end, I no longer felt satisfied. My experience of being unemployed had shown me that there were opportunities out there. I was beginning to believe that I was far less limited than I thought myself to be.

At home, I continued my meditation practice. Life had never felt so exciting. It was as though the larger purpose behind my unemployment was to force me (intentionally) to let go so that my world might open up. Without it, I would have continued to occupy my mind with things to manage, issues to strategize. As I paid attention to the details of these events, I became certain that whatever was happening, it was all working for my greater good.

In all of my experimenting with meditation, I became confident that I understood the technique. It was all about surrendering. It was harmless enough. Just surrender the thoughts, then surrender the fear of surrendering the thoughts. Let go, let go, let go. I felt completely powerless. There was no security, nothing solid to support me. I was getting good at this. I just continued to let go.

One morning as I sat in the dark letting go, surrendering, following nothing but the hum in the silence, I reached a point where there was nothing left to let go of. I was holding onto nothing. There was nothing left of me as I knew myself to be. I was just awareness watching the moments. As soon as I became aware that this was where I was, a switch was flipped in my consciousness, and my perception of the world was changed forever.

The screen of my mind became bright white. The whitest white imaginable. I could see nothing else. It was all around me. The hum of the silence was amplified. It had turned to a penetrating, piercing, ceaseless sound. It was not loud, just magnificently amplified, all inclusive. It happened simultaneously with the final surrendering as though I had crossed into a new realm, one that I could not cross by taking anything with me. At the same time, my entire body was filled with a feeling of unconditional love that was emanating from every fiber of my being. I had plugged into a circuit that ran on a very different current. That current had been running through me all along.

The experience was scaring me. It was an intense and mystical state, but I didn't want to break my connection with it. I sat there with it, in it, glowing from the vibration of total love, until I had to get ready for work. In all of that surrender, I was allowing the feeling of powerlessness. That willingness to let go pulled me behind the veil for a glimpse of the truly powerful.

I didn't know that was where any of this was leading. This wasn't in the manual. Meditation was packaged and sold to me as a habit that was good for me. A stress reducer. A sleep enhancer. I hadn't been searching for this. It found me. I thought I knew what religion had to teach. This went way beyond religion. Undoubtedly, this was an actual rendezvous with the divine.

I had simply knocked on the door with no clear picture of what I was looking for. Now, there was no denying that something was going out of its way to show me that there was much, much more going on here than I could have imagined.

Joan Enoch, M.D.

Born in New York, Joan Enoch went on to become a physician and psychiatrist/psychoanalyst. She is the mother of two sons, and a grandmother to six young adults. She considers herself a "wannabe" Buddhist, and a lifelong student of consciousness.

Her handle is justjoanthegypsy because of the places she has lived and travelled. She now finds herself living in Sequim, Washington on the beautiful Olympic Peninsula.

She has written on and off for thirty years and recently published a book of poetry, *Precarious Positions*.

Contact Joan at justjoan7740@gmail.com

BECOMING NOBODY/STAYING SOMEBODY

INVENTING A LIFE

It's not easy, daily inventing a life
Disparate and desperate elements meeting
in a semblance of cohesion
Mustering energy to believe, and have
others believe
That one's life marches with efficient and
rhythmic cadence
While through it all moves the jangling cacophony.
Only a semblance of sense, an external sense
of order holds it together
A sudden inner storm, a sigh, a tear starts the
heartbeat of change
The rockslide that can level the edifice.

I have often written poetry to cope with life. I created "Inventing a Life" some twenty-five years ago; I no longer remember why. But certainly an 'inner storm' was raging then as it does for many of us now. These are grim times for the world, I am sure far grimmer now than the summer I wrote "Inventing a Life."

These days, I need to write about coping in a time of multiple crises. Coping is important for all of us to master ... I know that from years as a psychotherapist. Now coping has bloomed into a life or death skill, because what is happening now can truly do us in. At the age of eighty, I am still 'the edifice' mentioned in the poem, but my foundation is cracking. I'm somebody on my way to being nobody. But I want to do it in my own way, with gladness as well as tears.

We started 2020 by being struck from behind with a great force; my partner Bob, his daughter and family, and I were hit, at 40 miles per hour, on New Year's Eve. We were slammed into the car ahead. Our car, that behemoth of metal, rubber, and glass, was destroyed. But we all walked out of that chariot; the little ones hardly remember it. Grateful doesn't begin to say it.

Maybe the fates were just toying with us, making us comfy with our good luck. But then, 2020 hit us with a lot of what it's got. I don't have to repeat it here. You all know it. We all have our version of it.

In one way or another, we all had to 'invent a life' in a short amount of time. In order to cope, we had to adapt by creating a structure that would leave us standing, the best we could. We had to muster 'energy to believe' that our lives marched on reasonably well, no matter the circumstances. But . . . we also had to grieve, rage, cry, and mourn openly for all of us and our planet.

Did I have the strength to invent that life, when even my 1995 self was almost ready to throw in the towel? Could this octogenarian figure out how to live, to survive, and even thrive in a very changed world?

Cacophony. What a word. The dissonance of politics, COVID-19, Black lives mattering, brutality, protests, counter-protests, ugliness, masks which make you almost unable to breathe even as they try to save you from your final breaths, fires everywhere in our beautiful west.

Today's reality is so much worse than when I wrote that poem. Can I gather up the strength to battle back? To do it, I must accept my negative feelings. Dealing with cacophony means finding energy every day. Creating intention. Finding an "internal sense of order."

I started with reflection. I looked through my poems of old, to see what I could make of them and figure if they could help me cope now. I published a collection of poetry during the first half of this difficult year. It was done by my birthday on July 7. *Precarious Positions* is not a book to sell but to give as a mini-memoir in poetic form. A print run of only one hundred, given to loved ones and dedicated individually. During the creation of this book, I may have raged at current events . . . but I was soothed. I coped.

I knew I would crash when it was done. That goes with the territory of big projects. How can I go on finding meaning in all this chaos? What prevails for the second half of this year? It often feels like my life is coming to an end. In a way, it is. There won't be any more work, or big projects. I am grieving. I am raging at injustice.

At the same time, I am also grateful for my good life. I am trying to curb my rage and do something useful. What that is I'm not always sure. Crying is OK. Anxiety and anger are justified. Grieving is necessary, but wallowing is not. I'm trying to learn an important lesson here, so of course I've written a poem about this situation. What will it tell me?

IN THE WORDS OF JOAN ENOCH, M.D.

SUFFERING

I'm suffering from ennui that I can't deny
I'm suffering from ennui and I don't know why
Can it be this country going down the tubes
Can it be our government and its assorted boobs
Can it be the warming of our planet dear
And all the folks around us living with the fear
Now of a pandemic decimating us, making us keep
Distances from those we even trust
Or could it be denial so close to us I say
Or those who'll die or suffer with so much moral decay
I think I know the answer to this riddle, yes
I'm suffering from ennui because I'm doing less.

Because I'm doing less. Ah! Being eighty can't be an excuse. One needs to keep moving. Maybe I can't march, but curling up in a fetal position is not allowed for long. Again, my coping mechanism is poetry . . . we all suffer, but not all the time. Write it out. Fight the instinct to fade. I say I want to become nobody so that I can easily disappear when the time comes, but I'm holding on to being somebody for dear life. Now when I say somebody, I don't mean SOMEBODY, (e.g., a famous person). It's enough to be justjoan, the gypsy, the good doc, the old earth mother. We all have these persona to keep — you know yours. I want to keep going as myself with poetic intensity, even in the face of all this chaos.

Can I do it? Can I be somebody intensely and still disappear with dignity, becoming nobody? Perhaps I can become nobody slowly, and not all at once. What an idea. Give up suffering when I can. Try to give up ennui. Use what I have written to help myself heal from 2020. You get the idea. The last line of the poem is important. Doing less can be very important when one was doing, perhaps, too much.

I will still rant on Facebook and to anyone who will listen. But I will also continue to cope by pushing the envelope of my creativity, by laughter, by cooking, and by swimming to soothe these old bones.

And I have added a new sort of poetry to my routine, just for the hell of it. I call them my Morning Mourning Poems. They will not bring me critical acclaim, but that is not their job. Each day when I awake, I start with a Morning Mourning burst to exorcize the ghosts, shake my fist at the universe, and begin my day.

IN THE WORDS OF JOAN ENOCH, M.D.

MORNING MOURNING POEMS

WE LIVE IN A TOWN

We live in a town
On the border...of insanity
I wish I could say
That it's all just profanity
The devil's in the details
I think is true
But literally, and sadly
It's increasingly the view
Human logic increases
Only up to a place
Where science can take us
And then we debase
Dumbing down is the answer
That simple minds find
To overwhelming complexity
That's just how the mind
Plays tricks on poor humans
Who can go no further
On the evolutionary scale

So sad I think I want to cry; but laughing hysterically
Instead I will (die, fry, lie, sigh, try)
Ah, yes - say Goodbye!

SMOKE GETS IN YOUR EYES

Yellow/greenish
Feeling squeamish
Inside/outside
Smoke I can't abide
And I feel fried
Cousins' phone call
Helps to break fall
Into some despair
And do we really dare
To have optimism
In the world's pessimism
This poor poem says yes
To the world's no.

IN THE WORDS OF JOAN ENOCH, M.D.

AT THE EDGE OF THE SEA

Oh boy. No instructions.
Find your own way
Some obstructions
Back away, many say
Must cross this pond
And while you're fond
Of this side
I say hit your stride
You have no choice
And so rejoice
In the way forward
Can't be a coward
Sink or swim
If it's your whim
To walk on water
Go for it.

ENDINGS

I want to get it right
In the middle of all this blight
I don't need to succeed
I wish to be freed
From self judgements and such
And the need to do much
I want to accept myself
Flawed and on the shelf
I want to be free
To just me be
I want to become nobody
While accepting the small somebody
Who tried in her time, which is passing
To help people strengthen and be lasting
Our ancestors are the base of our purpose
For all humanity to go safely into the future.

Melee McGuire

Melee McGuire is a high school counselor who grew up in New Zealand but happily settled in the Pacific Northwest seven years ago. She has published several short stories and her writing won the mystery category of the Pacific Northwest Writers Association in 2017, was a finalist in the romance category in 2019 and 2020, and was also a finalist in Contemporary Romance's 2020 Stiletto Competition and the 2020 Page Turner Awards. Melee is actively seeking an agent for her new book, *The Assassin's Guide to Internet Dating* and is working hard to make her dreams of becoming a full-time writer come true. She loves writing about fierce female assassins who dodge bullets, but never seem to escape Cupid's Arrow.

Follow Melee on the following accounts:
Instragram: meleemcguire
Twitter: @MeleeMcGuire
Facebook: Melee McGuire

JUST ANOTHER TUESDAY AFTERNOON IN 2020

The killing game was shifting. Sally adjusted her mask and pulled down the knit cap keeping her warm. The novel coronavirus shut down more than just businesses and schools. The assassination community was also experiencing unique challenges. Hired killers had to think outside of the pine box in a world where marks worked remotely and practiced social distancing.

It was a crisp day in the Pacific Northwest as wind whipped off the chilly waters of the Sound. Sally didn't often travel to Seattle, but she admired the contrast of nature's beauty and man's industry coexisting in the steel blue of buildings and burnt amber of fall leaves.

"Your mark should be approaching the hotel entrance." Richard's voice crackled in Sally's ear. She inadvertently flinched away from the newness of his gruff tone. He was so unlike her previous partner.

Sally worked with Penelope Briggs for fifteen years. They were a seamless team. Sally did the killing, Penelope handled intel and logistics. But Penelope did the stupidest thing a woman could do. She fell in love. While Sally begrudgingly approved of her friend's husband, she wasn't willing to commit to a happy ending for her friend. If Sally's life was any example, men were best left alone. But maybe Penelope would prove her wrong. Sally hoped she would. Especially now that Penelope was expecting. Twins. Sally shuddered. She would happily take on a Russian syndicate of crime bosses before tangling with offspring.

In an effort to be supportive, Sally agreed to let Penelope take a leave of absence. She refused to believe it was permanent, although Penelope continued to tell her that it was.

In an effort to make amends for her desertion, Penelope researched for a replacement with the same meticulous care she displayed when finding the appropriate double-stroller for her infants. She promised Sally that Richard was the absolute best. Sally trusted Penelope's opinion, but she still didn't trust Richard. He was an unknown factor and therefore a risk. It would take a few more years before she stopped double checking his work.

"Copy. I see him." Sally scanned the few pedestrians braving the wind and business shut-downs. A man wearing a black jacket, grey slacks, and green scarf moved with athletic grace on the empty sidewalk. His mask obscured any facial features with the exception of thick, black hair and dark eyes. "God, COVID really threw a wrench in the works, didn't it? Less people, but no way to really get a positive identification." Sally knew she was grumbling. But no crowds, social distancing, and heightened security made it so much harder to quickly and anonymously kill the assholes she was hired to eliminate.

She remembered with fondness the days when a girl could sidle up to a mark in a crowded bar, slip something nefarious into his drink, and skip away in the chaos of another business man having a 'sudden' heart attack. Now, everything was so much more complicated.

Of course, this job was never going to be simple, regardless of the international pandemic crippling the world. She wasn't just hired to kill the mark. She also needed to obtain documents in his possession. Documents detailing the formula and positive test results of a vaccine for this virus. A vaccine this man was selling to the highest bidder. A vaccine that belonged to all people. Her employer would ensure the vaccine and test results became available to the public.

She would have to gain access to his room, verify the documents were valid, kill him, and deliver the vaccine to her employer, thus saving the lives of millions. Just another Tuesday afternoon in 2020.

"Don't worry." Richard's graveled rumble interrupted her thoughts. "Our friend at SeaTac International Airport bugged him when he passed through security and got a positive I.D. I've been following him since then. That's your mark. Trust me." Richard sounded confident.

Sally wasn't so sure. She was glad the poppy-patterned mask she wore hid her smirk. She didn't trust Richard. Not yet. But she did trust his intel. Because she checked it herself.

"I'll follow him into the hotel lobby and pick up a copy of his key. You'll lose visuals on us until we're in his suite." Sally didn't usually talk this much on a job, but she was jumpy.

Richard was strategically holed up in the building adjacent to the hotel. He would have a clear view of Sally and the mark. If things went tits up, he could take out the man with one shot from his sniper rifle, hopefully. If sight lines were favorable, his aim was as good as his reputation, and no one moved when they shouldn't. It wasn't ideal, but that's why it was a back-up plan.

"Good luck." Richard's deep voice was amplified by the quiet city street.

"Luck is a poor substitute for skill and planning, Richard." Sally pulled the cap lower on her head and pushed through the door.

The concierge passed her a room key as she waited at the front desk. The room number was printed clearly in black ink. 2020. Fitting. The year had proven to be a disaster. Hopefully the kill would be less of a shit show.

Sally reached into her purse as she waited for the elevator to reach the top floor. The feeling of hard steel calmed her. Richard followed her instructions precisely and provided her with a Glock 19 that couldn't be linked back to an owner. She checked with her contacts, and he had conducted himself exactly as she directed. That was a good sign, but Sally wasn't yet convinced.

There were security cameras in the elevator, but for once, she didn't have to keep her face carefully angled away. With her cap and mask, it would be impossible for any bumbling detective to identify her later. Masks were a double-edged sword, making it harder for her to identify her mark, but so much easier to maintain anonymity. Protecting humanity from the virus by containing all of her respiratory droplets was another benefit, so she really didn't mind the new normal.

"I'm approaching the door. Do you have eyes on the mark?" Sally whispered.

"He's standing at the window. The briefcase is sitting on a table to his left." Richard's voice was steady, calm. Sally didn't want to admit that it helped to lower her racing heartbeat. After so many years in the game, nervousness seemed silly, but she always got jittery in the moments before a kill. It helped having a partner who stayed composed.

"Do you see any weapons?"

"None in clear view, but I can't see if he is armed. His jacket is still on."

"Copy. I'm going in." Sally pulled the Glock 19 from her purse and swiped the room key. The click of the door sounded like a cannon in her ear. She slipped through, kicking the door shut behind her. As it always seemed to do, time slowed and an odd peace descended, clear and cold. She raised her gun and aimed at the broad back of her mark.

"Keep your hands where I can see them and turn around." Sally pressed her lips together. She sounded like a cliché. She knew it and she hated it, but it was too late to change her words.

The mark turned around slowly. For the first time she got a clear view of his face. The calm evaporated.

"Hello, Sally. It's been awhile."

Sally almost didn't recognize her high school sweetheart. Fifteen years had added lines to his face and muscle to his frame.

"Shit." It was the first thought that came to mind and spilled so easily from her lips. In all her years as an assassin, she had never killed someone she knew. This was incredibly awkward.

"I don't suppose you would mind putting that gun down? Or at least, not aiming it at my heart?" He raised his eyebrows in a look she remembered from her past. It used to melt her into a gooey puddle. Now she stood frozen.

Sally blinked. Henry Smithson was her first love and the most stunning example of her romantic failures. He was the first man to hold her heart. He was also the first man to ruthlessly destroy it in the most simple and effective way.

Ghosting her the day after graduation. The morning after they slept together. Moments after she told him she loved him. The bastard. If she was going to kill anyone she knew, Henry was an excellent candidate.

"I can't possibly be aiming at your heart. You don't have a heart." As insults went, it was weak, but Sally was contending with a myriad of emotions that left little room for wit. "What the hell are you doing here? Actually, I don't care. It will be a real pleasure to shoot your sorry ass."

"Richard, you want to tell her, or should I?" Henry's smile was made more charming by the creases fanning from his obsidian eyes. Sally hated every distinguished line on his stupid face. Then his words registered.

"Richard? How do you know…" But she didn't need to finish the question. She knew. This was one big set up. And she'd walked into it like a total idiot. Her stomach turned to concrete. Acid burned up her esophagus. She should have trusted her instincts. Penelope was going to be so pissed when she realized her replacement got Sally killed.

"Sorry, Sally. I know this looks bad, but trust me." Richard's voice faltered.

"Trust you? Seriously?" Sally fired three shots into Henry's chest. Nothing happened. Because her gun was full of blanks. Because Richard had filled her gun with blanks. Because she was an idiot.

Sally threw the useless gun at Henry. He dodged the heavy weapon, and it crashed into the wall. Sally whipped a knife from her boot. "Fine. I was feeling a little conflicted about killing you, Henry, but I'm over it now. I'm looking forward to it. And Richard," she glanced out the window, hoping her new-ex-partner could see the promise in her eyes, "you're next."

Henry put his hands out in a calming gesture. "Sally, please. No one is going to die today."

"That's what you think." Sally snarled. He might outweigh her by a hundred pounds of muscle, but she was fast, skilled, and pissed.

"Sally, I need you."

Those were not the words she expected.

"Hah!" was her scintillating response. Sometimes actions were far more eloquent.

Sally leapt onto the bed, using the spring of the mattress to propel her across the room as she twisted in the air. She latched onto his back, her legs locking around his waist. She dug one hand into his thick hair, pulling his head back and exposing his neck. Gripping her knife, she pressed the cold blade against his throat.

"Richard, don't!" Henry spoke with command despite the sharp edge of Sally's knife digging into his skin. "I've got this."

Sally realized Richard's sniper rifle was aimed at her, not Henry. Her back-up plan was about to get Sally killed. Before she could swipe her blade across Henry's throat, he grabbed the wrist of her knife hand, twisting hard. She cried out. He moved faster than she expected. Pitching forward, he shucked her from his back. Sally slammed face first onto the floor. She tried to scramble away. But Henry was on her, holding her wrists to the carpet. He used his body weight to pin her beneath him.

"Sally, please. Just listen to me for a second."

Sally thrust up with her hips in a bid to move him, but the bastard didn't budge. She wriggled her legs, hoping to make enough space for her knee to find his groin, but Henry pinned her ankles with his feet, restricting her movements.

She was trapped. The biological reality of mass equaling mastery sucked balls.

"This is why I didn't just try to make an appointment with you. I knew you hadn't forgiven me. I knew you wouldn't be reasonable." Henry's voice was measured and calm.

"REASONABLE?" Sally's voice was less calm. "You broke my heart, you arrogant bastard! You were the first man I ever loved, and you left me with NO goodbye. No reason for abandoning me. Nothing. You're damned right I wouldn't meet with you. Not now. Not ten years from now, not when the earth hurtles off its axis and the human race disintegrates."

He shifted her wrists so that both were clasped in one of his hands. Slowly, he removed her mask.

Sally huffed out a breath. "You better not have a fever, or cough, or sore throat. We are way closer than six feet."

His fingers traced across her temple, down her cheek, his thumb grazing over her lips. "You are even more beautiful now than when I left."

Sally closed her eyes, refusing to let the pain in his gaze soften her. "But you still left, so I guess I wasn't beautiful enough, huh?"

"You had nothing to do with my leaving and everything to do with why I almost stayed."

"It doesn't matter." Sally lied. "That was a million years ago, and I was a different person." She willed the ache in her chest to subside. "What do you want, Henry?"

Henry opened his mouth to say something then seemed to change his mind. He clamped his mouth shut. His jaw muscles jumped, and Sally tried not to notice how firm his lips were when he pressed them together. He shook his head, sighed then started over. "You can probably surmise that I don't have a vaccine for this virus. There isn't one. But in a few days, a vaccine won't matter. COVID-19 was just a test run."

Sally's brows drew together. "What do you mean? Test run for what?"

"To see how the world would react. How quickly systems would respond to the threat. How governments, hospitals, hell, even how people would behave. And based on the data, we all sucked pretty hard."

"So, what? What does that mean?"

"It means the test-run proved we are not ready for a viral pandemic. My employers are confident a deadlier version of COVID will prove remarkably successful in killing off at least seventy percent of humanity."

Henry shifted, slowly raising his body off her. Sally should have been able to breathe easier without his weight pressing on her chest, but she was struggling to get air in her lungs. "Why? And how can they possibly do this?"

"The why is easy. We are overpopulated. The world cannot continue to sustain human life at our current rate of growth. Certain people want to ensure they control who dies, and who survives in a new, much more sparsely populated world where all of the resources belong to the remaining thirty percent of humanity."

"Well, shit." Sally shook her head. Her mind wanted to reject the logic, but powerful people would do insane things to protect their supremacy.

"Yes. Exactly. Deep shit."

"How do you know about this?"

"When I left the military, I went into the private sector, working for a biotechnology company funded by a small group of very wealthy men. I thought we were going to be using our research for gene therapy. I was wrong. So wrong."

"So this biotech company is going to release a new, more deadly virus?" Sally controlled her voice so he couldn't hear her fear.

"Yes. And only the very wealthy and very powerful will have access to a vaccine that will keep them immune. I need your help to stop this virus before it's released, Sally."

Sally sat up. She'd lost her cap in the scuffle and she raked shaky fingers through her hair. "Why? Why me?"

"Because you know how to kill people. And we need to kill some very dangerous people." Henry kept his gaze steady on her.

She was living in a nightmare populated by insidious assholes with biological weapons, and her ex-boyfriend was her only potential ally. "2020 is the absolute *worst*. I thought we had met our quota for bad shit that can happen in one year."

"Will you help me? Help us?" Henry held his breath, waiting for her reply. He used to hold his breath whenever he wanted something badly.

"Please, Sally." Richard's voice crackled through her ear bud. She'd almost forgotten about him.

Sally thought about Penelope and the twins. "So if we do this, we'll be saving the lives of millions?"

"Hundreds of millions."

Sally sighed. "So we have to find these guys, kill them, destroy the virus, and thwart the most powerful members of our society, thus saving hundreds of millions of people. Just another Tuesday afternoon in 2020."

Terry Sager

I have always been drawn to mysteries and psychological thrillers. Alfred Hitchcock movies were my favorites. In my writing, I am fascinated by the human psyche, especially the dark side. I was so intrigued by the human mind that I studied Psychology and obtained my Bachelor of Science degree in Psychology from Virginia Tech. I am a member of the Pacific Northwest Writers Association.

My dog and I enjoy exploring the wilderness where my imagination sometimes works against me when I hear a strange noise coming from the forest. When not writing or exploring, I volunteer at a local animal rescue.

Contact Terry at terrysagershuck@gmail.com

COVID, CAMPING AND COPING

Even those of us who have been spared a direct hit from the COVID-19 pandemic have been grief-stricken by the enormity of loss of life and livelihood. None of us has been spared the collateral damage of losing the simple freedom of going about the activities that made up our daily lives. These were the things that served as respite from our obligations. If our escape was outside the confines of our homes, COVID-19 took it from us.

RV camping with my dog, Cricket, was my main escape. I had only been doing it about a year when the virus crept in and unapologetically snatched it away. The main reason I started to RV was to avoid that day of regret—the day when maybe I wouldn't be physically *able* to venture out on my own and experience nature's beauty and the peace. I never expected a pandemic to stop me.

I was an RV novice and since my co-pilot was a dog, if (when) anything went wrong, I would have to handle it myself. If I overthought it, I would never do it. Feel the fear, and do it anyway. But what was I afraid of? Sometimes the mundane, like backing over a picnic table, person, or cliff when maneuvering into a campsite, or having the dump site experience go terribly wrong. In general, screwing up and being humiliated. Visions of long-timers staring, pointing and laughing at me haunted my thoughts. And then there was the big fear. Fear of the dark.

In early February, 2020, still blissfully ignorant that the tsunami called COVID-19 was rolling in, I went to a campground that was basically deserted. I was so happy when I got there and realized there were only about five other RVs in the park. Then it got dark.

Around 8 p.m. I took Cricket out one last time. Flashlight in one hand, leash in the other, I led her toward a grassy area behind the RV. Cricket started barking and lunging toward something in the dark. I looked in that direction and saw a light, like an L.E.D. lantern. I didn't see anyone, but she continued her "danger bark." Someone *had* to be holding the lantern, but whoever it was didn't say a word. I wasn't about to shine my flashlight on them and demand, "Who goes there?" It scared me, big time.

I scrambled back into the RV, pulling Cricket, who was still straining on the leash and still barking. With visions of the bogeyman, I turned off the lights in the RV, and peeped out a window. At first, I saw nothing. After a very long five minutes, I saw the light go up the road and disappear into the woods. Maybe someone had come to the campground late and was making their way back from the restrooms.

Since it was February, I had eleven hours until daylight. And I had no cell service. I really had no choice but to try to sleep and tell myself it was nothing. I slept, eventually, with the lights on and the curtains closed. That was *true* fear. I still can't figure out why the person didn't just say something, instead of standing there in silence.

At daybreak, I walked toward that campsite, just to confirm my hypothesis that it was a latecomer the night before. It was vacant. To this day, I do not have a reasonable explanation for that one. I did add a couple self-protection devices and motion-sensor lights. It can be a little scary when they activate if you have a mind like mine that is full of true-crime stories. But so far, the only culprits have been leaves blowing across the ground.

So, when I thought I was ready to enjoy nature off the proverbial grid, and camp by a river or lake with no one around (like those RV ads I saw on TV), I realized I had to conquer my fear of the evil things that may, or may not, lurk in the dark. I knew the boogeyman would be watching from the woods as I found that perfect isolated spot by the lake and set up camp. He'd wait for the cover of darkness to make his move. Oh, how I wished I'd never read a Stephen King novel or watched an episode of true crime on the Investigation Discovery channel! Why, oh why hadn't I read romance novels and watched Rom-Coms?

Fear of COVID-19 was similar, because of the unknowns. But I wasn't as afraid of Mr. Virus as I was of a pitch-black night in the woods. It seemed like no one could really agree on what was happening with this virus, and maybe it would all be over soon. It was easy to be in denial—a wonderful way of coping, at first. I'll have to try denial the next time I go camping and am afraid of what might be hanging out in the shadows. But, maybe like COVID-19, there *is* something to fear.

Mid-March 2020, just before COVID-19 closures, I returned from a trip, thinking about the next two trips I had before school was out, and the summer crowds made RVing too frantic for my taste. Within a few days, the stay at home order was announced. *Okay, wow, but it's just two weeks, no big deal. I can do that.* Then the order was extended and more closures were announced. It was going to be a bit more serious than I expected, but probably over by Easter. I was pretty sure I would still be able to go on my spring trips. Denial was still with me.

Then I started receiving emails that cancelled my April camping reservations. Then May. And not just campgrounds were closing, forest lands and other federal and state-managed lands, were closed to camping. If you can't even be out in nature without fear of a virus, then this is real. And with all the angst in the world, I was angry I couldn't go camping. I lost my main coping mechanism, and I was powerless to do anything about it. But certainly, it would be over by July. Denial, again.

However, the numbers of COVID-19 cases and deaths increased daily. Anxiety crept in because it wasn't clear if even experts knew what they were talking about. What were we supposed to believe? Cancellations continued. The daily count of lost lives, lost jobs, and lost dreams began to pile up. People on TV were working from home, mumbling through masks. At least Walmart and Safeway were open. But for how long? Would there be food shortages?

COVID-19 left us very little choice. Even if we hadn't been aware of it, we had been going through some of the stages of grief: denial, anger and depression. We were about to enter the last phase: acceptance.

In an RV, you're self-contained. You bring your own supplies. But, if you don't have hook ups to electricity and water at a campground, you are on your own to gauge how long your RV battery and water tank will serve you. You need to know, or suffer the consequences. It *makes* you understand how electricity works. It definitely increases your awareness of your usage of power and water. It changes your consumption habits. If you can get this, you can stay out in the "wild." So, you learn. On the road, I learned something new each time. Luckily, my first trip was problem free, but no one gets away with that for long.

Several months earlier, at 2 a.m. the carbon monoxide alarm went off in my RV. My interior lights wouldn't come on, so I suspected a battery failure. The only thing I could see was the menacing red light on the alarm telling me it was horribly upset. Did I know where I had put the flashlight? I pushed every button I could find to turn off the brain-splitting shriek, not finding the right one for what seemed an eternity. I was sure it had woken up the entire campground, and was seriously thinking I may just have to take a hammer to the damn thing. (I put a hammer on my list for the next trip.) I also made sure I kept the flashlight within reach from then on.

The alarm was activated, not because there was a leak, but because my RV battery had indeed died. The battery shouldn't have been dead, and denial did not change the facts. I finally pushed the right button, and the noise stopped. Now, at least, I could peel Cricket off the ceiling. An hour later she quit trembling. As I sat on the edge of the bed in the dark, I wondered what to do next. I had no power. It was now 3 a.m. I decided to lay down and try to sleep. The Pollyanna side of my brain said, "Hey! At least you have *propane* heat!" Then the Freddy Krueger side said, "Think about it, dumb ass. You have propane heat, but no electricity to run the blower motor. Still happy?" The last thing I wanted to do was ask for advice, but it looked like that was what I was going to have to do in the morning. I had five hours of waiting, and that's when, in the middle of a very dark night, I learned "acceptance." And not for the last time.

On the next trip, I was awakened by wind gusts buffeting the RV. Why do these things happen at 2 a.m.? I started to feel a bit of anxiety coming on as the wind rocked the RV. I remembered news footage of tractor-trailers flipping over on the interstate during a windstorm. I looked out a window and no one else in the campground was panicking. Maybe they were still asleep? I laid in bed wondering how much wind speed it takes to topple an RV. The dog was still asleep, so maybe we were okay. Wouldn't a ranger, or whoever runs these places, warn us if we were in danger? Or is that just on TV, too?

I did the research later on how much wind it takes to topple an RV, installed an app on my phone that would give me wind speed alerts, and added that to my ever growing "toolbox."

The big lesson was acceptance. Again. It wouldn't be the last time I told myself, "There is nothing you can do about it right now. You can worry all night and lose sleep, or you can trust that it will be okay, somehow. And when the sun comes up, you will figure it out. You can handle this." And it wouldn't be the last time Freddy chimed in with maniacal laughter: "No! You *cannot* handle this. You just wait and see!"

Another extension to the stay at home order and another camping cancellation email arrived. And more people died. Denial finally died too. I began to simply accept the closures and the stay at home extensions as the new reality. I watched the news for updates and if I watched TV at all it was re-runs that took me back to a normal time. I was still saddened every day by the stories of people who lost their loved ones and their livelihoods, but I reached my limit of what I could take in. I couldn't just grab my dog, and head out to nature, RV or not, because trails were closed. A vague heaviness settled in: depression.

Some restrictions were relaxed. Campgrounds began to open slowly. Very slowly. Most campgrounds that took reservations were full months ago, and people who had lost their reservations to COVID-19 (like me) would have to hustle to find a campsite. I'm not big on hustling—it sounds very stressful to drive around for hours, looking for a campsite, in a crammed campground. Although disappointed, I accepted that my escape was going to be in my back yard for the summer, and was grateful to have that.

Looking back, I can see that even my RV escapades weren't really an escape; there was always something to deal with. The RV was the vehicle that transported me to the places I could immerse myself in the beauty of nature and to stay long enough to absorb its power of rejuvenation. I am forever grateful to those before me who had the foresight to preserve it. I was able to take a trip at the end of the summer of 2020, and was reminded of my favorite quote by the naturalist, John Muir: "Into the forest I go, to lose my mind and find my soul." Well said, Mr. Muir, well said.

Al Kitching

I am a retired lawyer who mostly practiced as a public defender. My wife and I moved to the Olympic Peninsula about two years ago from Bainbridge Island. Since moving here, to what seems pretty close to paradise, we've become part of a neighborhood writing group which has been a great impetus for me to venture into poetry writing.

Contact Al at all.thewords@olypen.com

RELAX

"Relax," the Sage told me, smiling, "relax—just relax. "
Relax?!?
Most of my moments
I'm gripping tightly to the edges
Of what seems to be me,
In thrall to three or four of my 10,000 thoughts.

Even so, now — so I hear — added to the 10,000 thoughts,
Are 10,000 "friends"
That beckon through the ether,
Media sirens admonishing and beseeching unceasingly,
Luring us, like Ulysses, to the shoals between truth
and desire,
With no mast to bind ourselves to,
Nor the will to apply the necessary wax to the ears
of our mind,
We sail heedlessly into the mobius loop of infinite babble,
Our repeating narratives ever continuing
Until death finds us,
Forever unreconciled
To the living missed.

RUSSIAN ROULETTE CRAPSHOOT

In this Russian Roulette crapshoot of COVID-19,
old adages speak ignored wisdom to our social unraveling:
COVID-19 is the duck that walks and quacks like a duck;
climate change is the chicken who, at long last,
comes home to roost.

Simple parables vie with our ability, gifted to humans,
to hear our desires untethered from consequences,
science twisted into chosen falsity to suit politics and power,
"truth" bandied about like a tennis ball in a match of life
and death.

Though all are vulnerable,
unmasked exhalations from behind defiant eyes
demand "freedom" to risk any and all with their breath,
such human guns breathe bullets of pestilence,
everyone connected by virus-ridden air,
crossing all boundaries,
all cultures,
proximities and distances
Inextricable.

RAVEN DANCE

Once upon a time, my wife and I were visiting one of the islands hereabouts. We were driving down an empty road, about a half mile into tree-covered meadowed land. It was a hot summer day, so we had the car windows down. The sun broke through the shadows of the trees on either side of us. Then, we heard a great commotion of raven talk to our right. Being quite partial to ravens, we pulled off the road. I turned the engine off and we listened. We heard what sounded like several disputing ravens forcefully expressing themselves with loud confident caws—not the usual varied and subtle croaks and chuckles and other gentle clucking crooning liquid raven speech we often hear where we live.

We quietly walked into the forest that extended past our sight. About twenty yards from our car, in what looked like a small and deserted corral lit brightly with sunlight, we saw three ravens dancing, facing each other in a circle, hopping, bowing and circling, raising themselves a foot or more off the ground, their wings bowed and flexed, primary feathers extended. Light brown corral dust rose glowing into the sun's beams as they moved and cawed, wings and beaks open, heads poised and cocked, circling and bowing to each other. The ravens' movements and energy seemed akin to the energy, power, grace and earth/sky connectedness of the celebratory dances of Native Americans, complete with chanting. This scene was magically evocative, summoning ancient images and feelings beyond my merely human ken.

Suddenly, from the trees overlooking the corral, there exploded raven caws that seemed to exhort the dancers—a cheering section or soundtrack for this raven ritual to which the dancers seemed to reply. We watched for a few minutes, awed and humbled to witness our kindred's communal ritual. At some point, perhaps because one of the ravens saw or otherwise sensed us, the cheering stopped and the three dancers leaped up together, their powerful wings whooshing loudly in the now silent air, driving the corral's dust into the waning sunlight. Their large dark forms quickly disappeared into the shadow-mottled trees.

We looked at each other, shaking our heads in stunned amazement, feeling great gratitude for the fortune that allowed our path to synchronize with the ravens' tribal celebration. Curious, we walked about thirty feet to the small, about a hundred-foot square corral, abandoned and beginning to be absorbed by the land. What *was* this about — what were the ravens doing? What were they saying? Being great imitators, were they imitating Native American dances they had observed? Or did the ancient ravens teach the First Peoples to dance?

We know that ravens speak to each other. We hear their speech most days where we now live. Recent research has identified eighty distinct raven calls/sounds, with regional dialects and variations. Given that we now have raven neighbors, I've been trying to learn their speech, quite difficult for this human, though occasionally I think the raven(s) respond to my clumsy attempts — by laughing. Ravens are great mimics and like to play, sliding down like otters and human children, snow banks on their backs and aerial cavorting that puts the Blue Angels to shame.

Jennifer Ackerman, in her book *The Genius of Birds*, notes the talent birds have for "catching on" to their surroundings and exploiting them. For all the belittling of "bird brains," she shows them to be uniquely impressive creatures within their own evolutionary contexts. Regardless of the increased understanding of "bird brains," their complexity, sophistication and power, what remains with me from those moments is a great wonder and respect for our feathered kin, and deep gratitude for the privilege of seeing them dance.

JADE TREES

Some Jade Trees are so rare
as to fetch $1000 a plant.
Others are guarded as family heirlooms,
a family's prosperity stretching back in time
to that first water filled leaf,
fallen to root in uncertain soil,
each new leaf a coin of the realm,
prosperity and fortune across ages.

Most Jade Trees are as rare as you and me,
grown from our common dirt,
green leaves paired,
opposable,
butterfly wings poised —
to fly,
to fall,
stitching heaven
and earth
together.

Heidi Hansen

At an early age, I learned the power of words. Given an option, I will always choose an essay test over True/False. My footing in journalism side-stepped into marketing. After a career marketing high tech products and services, I became an entrepreneur, first operating a gift basket business in Silicon Valley, then as a Realtor in the Pacific Northwest. All along the way, writing was the common thread, weaving words to create an idea or portray a product.

Three books of my short stories have been published, *A Slice of Life*, *A Second Slice*, and *BitterSweet*. I co-founded Olympic Peninsula Authors in 2016, and edited their four volumes of anthologies, *In The Words Of Olympic Peninsula Authors*. I am also a member of Northwest Independent Writers Association (NIWA) and a contributor to their 2019 anthology.

Contact Heidi at heidi@olypen.com

IN THE ZONE

I took on adult responsibility when I was eleven in order to stay up late. In the 1960s *The Twilight Zone* aired Friday nights at nine. I'd jump into my father's recliner as he climbed the stairs to bed. "Don't forget," he'd say, "take out the dog, turn off the lights and be quiet." Everyone else retired earlier. I was the last one up.

I'd adjust the volume as Rod Serling took center stage, and I sat at rapt attention, often pulling a pillow over my face to hide the scarier moments. When the show reached its conclusion and Rod signed off, the heebie-jeebies magnified for me. First I had to wrangle the sleeping terrier and shoo her outside to the porch. Then I'd turn off the lights. All of the lights. We lived in a hundred-year-old farmhouse full of odd-shaped rooms and mysterious sounds. There were no two-way light switches. I ascended the creaking staircase in the dark. Several treads squealed when you stepped on them. I'd climbed those stairs so many times, I knew to keep to the outside to avoid the creaks and groans, more to calm my nerves than worry about waking the rest of the family. At the top of the staircase, I turned right and negotiated the dorm room where three of my sisters slept, hoping no toys lay in my path, then through the door into the bedroom I shared with my sister. Quietly I disrobed, slipped into my pajamas and bed. It seemed that hours passed before sleep. Remnants of the show tricked me into imagining sounds and shadows that played on the walls. The pine tree, taller than the house, swept its branches against the windows making me jump.

In one episode of *The Twilight Zone* an old woman was disturbed by sounds of something in her attic. She climbed the stairs carrying a broom. There in her clean attic were miniature humanoids scurrying about and attacking her. She did her best to sweep them away. It was not until the camera panned that you saw their tiny spaceship and the stars and stripes insignia. I was trying to sleep in my bed only two feet from the door to our attic. The sound of the tree branches was reminiscent of her sweeping the broom, and the imagined mice I heard scratching in the walls were like the spacemen.

My favorite episode on *The Twilight Zone*, the one that always unnerved me was the one where the "ugly" person went under the plastic surgeon's knife to have her face reshaped to normal. You never saw a face during the entire show until the final unveiling. Then the tables were turned because the surgery was deemed a failure, but she was beautiful by our standards, but not their normal. And to think, I took this roller coaster ride every Friday night.

In college I had the opportunity to meet Mr. Serling in person and had him sign his latest book, *Night Gallery*. He died the following year. Through the intervening years, I've moved many times, each time paring down my book collection, but I still have that one.

A few years ago, my friend Tobias told me that he met someone who claimed to have several scripts written by Rod Serling for *The Twilight Zone*, I invited myself along for a look see. I hoped it was true, and that I might be able to purchase one.

Tobias and I arrived amid a throng of fans. The odds that we would even make it into the house were disappearing as more and more cars arrived. But the purveyor recognized Tobias and waved us through the garden gate around to the back of the house. There, many collectors were bidding for this episode or that, but he handed a manila envelope to Tobias. "For you," he said. "It never made it to the screen." Tobias reached for his wallet, but was told. "No, this is yours." He smiled at me, then dismissed himself.

We headed back to Tobias' car where we opened the envelope and pulled out a sheaf of papers. The edges were slightly curled and yellowed as they should be to reflect the years since the show had aired. He held the pages between us, and we scanned them hungrily. I would nod when I was ready for the next page. We were taken with the story until it ended. More accurately, there were no more pages. The story was left up in the air. No resolution. No irony. No moral.

Tobias kept the script for some time then mailed it to me. I set it aside. But as of late I wanted a reread, so searched my bookshelves until I found it.

The story was a Serling specialty about a world civilization that suddenly came to a screaming standstill. It was reminiscent of our questions about what happened to the people of Easter Island or the Incas. The characters in the story included a round table of world-famous scientists who were faced with a global pandemic. As they grappled with a way to save the people, another problem presented itself, then another, until it took on the proportions of the book of Revelations.

After the toilet paper scare, the forests of the world were ignited by lightning storms, then came the hurricanes, the typhoons, the tornadoes, and the killer hornets that circled the globe. When they descended from the skies, they were not killing the people, but they ate through the crops eliminating grains. Then the skies opened, and torrential rains fell, causing flooding. Yet the pandemic still plagued them. Governments blamed one another then tried to cooperate against a common enemy. But there the story stopped.

What would Hollywood do with this story? Probably the same as on *Dallas* when Bobby suddenly came back from the dead in the shower, or Bob Newhart would wake in the night to tell Suzanne Pleshette about his crazy dream of running an inn in Vermont. Or better yet, that moment when it was revealed that the entire story of *St. Elsewhere* was only in the imagination of the autistic son of Donald Westphall who was not a doctor after all, but a construction worker.

What did Rod Serling know about 2020? How could he have imagined this? Or should we take a page from Hollywood and go back to bed and hope to wake to a different reality?

CLOSE QUARTERS

"Is that new?" her husband of many years asked.

She looked at him "This?" she questioned tugging on the hem of her nightgown.

"No, the pan," he pointed to what she washed in the sink. She looked down. "This?"

He nodded. "I don't remember seeing it before."

Thoughts swirled in her head. *How would he see it? He didn't cook, and he didn't wash up after she cooked. We've been quarantined for nearly a year, and I've prepared three meals a day — every day. That's a hell of a lot of meals.*

She tried to calculate the number of days multiplied by three, but the numbers were too big to work in her head. She'd need a calculator. Remembering his question, she turned back to him. "You don't remember this? You gave it to me for Christmas last year."

"Oh yeah," he said with no recollection. He turned to go.

"And when are you going to get a haircut?"

He ran his hand through his hair absentmindedly. "What? I need a haircut?"

"At least a trim. Are you trying for a ponytail?"

"I've never had a ponytail." He reached up and pulled the hair off his neck fashioning a ponytail with his hand. "My hair has never been this long before."

"Well . . ."

He was half listening. "What?" he asked, still fussing with his ponytail. Maybe in another month, he could ask her to braid it. Visions of Willy Nelson danced in his head.

"Are you going to get a haircut?" She called out after him.

"I don't think so."

"Just get it trimmed up. You look like a mad scientist. What's the one we've been watching on TV? Oh yeah, Alfred Einstein."

"Albert Einstein," he muttered as he went in search of a rubber band for his ponytail.

Later, she started again. "When you get a haircut, you know you'll have to make an appointment. There's no more walk-ins."

He sighed wondering why she was nagging him about his hair. In fact, he couldn't remember them ever discussing his hair before. The next words tumbled from his mouth without thinking. "Are those pants new?"

She looked down at her slip-on sweatpants. "Not new," she said flecking at the paint stain on the right thigh. "Why would you think they were new?"

"Seemed a bit tight."

He watched the color rise in her cheeks and maybe a tear in her eye, but he turned away quickly and scuttled back to his desk. *I think I hit a nerve.*

She slammed the bedroom door. *What the hell? And yes, they are a bit tight. Everything is a bit too tight. Including our close quarters.* She threw herself on the bed and sobbed. "When will this be over? When will we get back to normal?"

That was when they realized they had hit upon a topic that would send the other away. A natural selection for distancing when some breathing space was needed.

A few months before the pandemic, they had sold their home of many years and downsized to a tiny house set on a rural quarter-acre of land. Their plan was to bankroll their retirement years with the proceeds and live meagerly until then. After all, how much room did they need? He worked for a high tech firm and was usually on the road one or two weeks each month; she was a homemaker involved with a variety of charitable organizations. There were always bake sales, garage sales, and fund-raising events to be organized and worked. How much time did they actually spend at home together?

That question was answered in early March. Like a race car, their time together sped up from "nearly zero" to "every minute" with the turning of a single page on the daily calendar. At first it was fun, like a honeymoon. But now, the togetherness was wearing thin. Distancing oneself from the other became a necessity.

Their tiny house was tiny. There were only two doors; the front door and the bedroom door. His office was set up in the living room area at their dining counter. Unless she was in the bedroom, she was within an arm's distance of him. And vice versa. She began retiring earlier each evening and rising before dawn. He took the night shift, staying up into the wee hours and sleeping till noon. In being so close, neither could do anything without the other seeing and commenting.

Early on in these days at home, she made herself a schedule: laundry on Monday, shopping on Tuesday, vacuuming on Wednesday, etc. Then bored with the routine, she reverted to doing what needed to be done when she felt like it. Her calendar and clock were reset to whenever.

He, of course, remembered her schedule. "I thought laundry was Monday – it's Thursday, you know," he said watching her open the cabinet that housed their tiny washer/dryer unit.

"Of course I know it's Thursday. I just feel like doing laundry today." She stuffed the meager pile of clothing into the washer.

"In fact, you forgot to do laundry last week," he said.

"Think about it. You wear your pjs all day and so do I. Last week I don't think we ever got dressed."

He laughed. "But I did put on a shirt when I Zoomed for client meetings."

"That's right. I threw a scarf around my neck rather than get dressed for a Skype call."

"Another advantage of this pandemic, our clothes will last longer."

"Or the fact that I can't keep my new year's resolution," she said.

"What was that?"

"I wasn't going to buy any new clothes this year. A cost cutting plan."

"Well, aren't you keeping to it?"

"So far, but. . ."

"What?"

"The reason I don't get dressed is because nothing fits."

"So, buy some new clothes. We've cut costs in other places. You deserve a new outfit now and again," he offered.

"Thank you. That was nice of you to say."

"Have you any idea where the hole punch is?" he asked.

He stood at the counter fussing with his belt.

"What are you doing?"

"I need another hole in this belt, can't keep my pants up."

If her clothes were getting tighter, his seemed to be looser. It wasn't fair. She did all the shopping and all the cooking. Why was he benefiting, and she was not? She turned away, lost in thought. *It just doesn't make sense. We're eating healthier and better than ever. No fast food. But my clothes are getting smaller, tighter. Must be the dryer.*

When she did the wash, she separated her clothes from his. Certainly not enough for a load in either case. She washed hers in cold water, his in hot; then dried hers on low heat, and his on high. The results were the same. For the next week she limited herself to half his portion at meals.

Several weeks passed. She bought fresh vegetables and prepared tasty and healthy meals. Three times a day. She served herself half as much as him and allowed him seconds whenever he wanted. His clothes were washed in hot water and dried on high heat; hers in cold water and low heat. Finally, the tide turned. His pants were a little tighter and hers looser. Another month and she was feeling good about getting her weight under control. And with that attitude change, she was slamming the bedroom door and flailing on the bed less. She decided to do some rearranging of their clothing.

Of course, in a tiny house there is no walk-in closet, but there was a small hanging space, and they each had two drawers. Looking into his drawers she realized that these were not the newer clothes she purchased when they moved. She had replaced all his socks and underwear with new, bought him new shirts and jeans. The old clothes were put in a box to be donated. But somehow the new clothes box and the old clothes box must have been switched. *Good thing I never got around to donating that*, she thought.

A quick wash and the new clothes were put away where they should have been. This time the old clothes went into the trunk of her car to donate or toss.

The next time he dressed, he exclaimed that his clothes were a bit tighter and he had better ramp up his exercise and decrease his consumption. She smiled and suggested they get their bicycles out and start riding.

And in that way they trained for the annual bicycle race, dropped another size and lived happily ever after in their tiny house. You may see them riding on the Discovery Trail. You'll recognize him by the long gray braid down his back.

Jan Thatcher Adams, M.D.

Dr. Jan was blessed to have a forty-seven-year career in medicine practicing womb to tomb needs, and delivering over 3,000 babies. She treasures these years and misses the patients and staff deeply.

Throughout her career, she also pursued humanitarian goals — clowning in many countries and refugee camps with Dr. Patch Adams, and providing medical care to unserved multitudes in many countries, including Haiti, Argentina, and Nepal. She developed and managed a charity and art gallery for the benefit of Russian orphans.

She is the author of two published books, *Football Wife*, and *From The Beating Heart of Healing*, both available through Amazon.

In retirement, she continues her interests in music, art, and writing, especially story telling. She resides in Port Angeles, Washington with her husband and three cats.

Contact Jan at jantadams@aol.com

DEATH IN THE TIME OF SOCIAL DISTANCING

It was expected. Blindness and dementia had, unrelentingly, reduced her life to bed only, puréed food, total care for over two years. She had wished to die for a few years. And then she refused to eat, let the food slide from her mouth, would not swallow. Barely conscious, she continued like this for eight days.

At 10:45 pm my husband, her loving son, checked on her and found her in this usual state. At 11 pm, I checked on her. She was gone — finished with this torture her life had become, nine days before her 89th birthday. Far from her homeland, Russia.

We had cared for her without hospice or home nursing. My MD medical abilities guided us in whatever needed done. But that meant we had to proceed in a different way, now. Especially since the world outside our home had turned upside down due to COVID-19.

We had notified the funeral home a few days earlier of her nearing her expected end. It was required, since no other personnel had been witnessing her decline. Now, we were instructed to call the sheriff, who came to confirm circumstances. Followed by EMTs, who placed EKG leads to demonstrate no heartbeat. Followed by a chaplain who was required to stay in our home until the funeral home came to take Jenya away. A kind former ER associate agreed to sign her death certificate.

Three hours later the funeral folks arrived. My deeply grieving husband asked questions — would they be washing her body? (A custom in Russia). No, they would not. Could he visit her each day until cremation? No, he could not; the funeral home was closed to visitors.

And so Jenya left our home in a brightly-colored body bag. And my husband was left to grieve without any of his customs that might bring comfort.

There could be no gathering the next day to celebrate and honor her astonishing life, a life of courage and humor lived through the worst of World War II and the soviet years. There could be no gathering at the funeral home for the cremation. There would be no gatherings at the marking of the three Russian traditional rings the soul passes through on the journey to heaven — gatherings at days ten, forty, and one year.

Instead, the funeral home called some days later to announce Jenya's ashes were ready for pickup. My husband was instructed to call from his car when he reached their parking lot, and they would bring the ashes out to him.

All over the world, survivors are suffering the loss of loved ones, while tragically unable to perform the comforting and completing rituals that aid the grief process. Loved ones are just gone. No final words, no final caresses, no comforting rituals. Death as part of the continuum of life — suddenly no longer something loved ones can participate in.

The planet has suffered this before, in plague and war and despotic regimes.

In time, the wounded spirit of humanity will emerge again, to celebrate the lives of our lost loved ones, and rejoice in a renewed and refreshed view of our blessings.

RHONDA

It is yearly exam time,
she is a many-year patient.

I take her history —
feeling fine.
Her exam is normal, too.

As she sits on the exam table,
completely swathed in
paper sheet and gown,
we have end of the visit conversation.

This discussion tips topsy,
when completely off the subject
she asks if I would like to be her special friend.
I understand from her body language
and unusual format of her question —

she is inviting me into a sexual relationship.
This is a first in my exam rooms.

With a few exceptions,
I have not had any kind
of personal friendship
with a current patient.
Let alone this suggestion.

IN THE WORDS OF JAN THATCHER ADAMS, M.D.

I am kind in my definite "no,"
and once again,
I realize I will never see or hear
all possible situations
in my profession.

JENNIFER

She is here again,
every Wednesday.
She has a psychiatric disorder,
undiagnosed.
She refuses to see
a psychiatrist.

Instead, she angrily stalks
into my office every week,
demanding soothing words
and gentle direction.

Of course her life is messy.
She seems to think this is my fault.
She scowls at me throughout
the visit.

I admit I groan when I see her name
on my appointment list.
She appears to hate me,
even murderously so.

And yet, here she is,
every week.

IN THE WORDS OF JAN THATCHER ADAMS, M.D.

One night I came home to my
secluded country dwelling,
to find her standing, partially hidden,
in the woods.

I felt fear, and called the sheriff.
He picked her up without incident.
The next day I dictate the letter
releasing her as my patient,
providing many options for her care.

I don't ever see her again, but
find myself wary for
some years.

JOSHUA

He enters the ER
Reclining, moaning,
Clearly ill.

He is young — 37.
His belly hurts him terribly.
He states "I haven't been able
to poop for 6 months."

This constipation complaint
is common in the ER,
but something is different here.

"I've lost 30 pounds,
I can't eat.
I really can't poop.
I've told several doctors,
but enemas and laxatives just make
the pain worse."

On exam, his belly is hard and tender.
CT exam is tragic.
He has advanced colon cancer,
spread throughout.

IN THE WORDS OF JAN THATCHER ADAMS, M.D.

I now have to tell him this
truly terrible news.
In our conversation, I note how
young he is, and ask if
anyone has colon cancer in his family.

"Yeah, my dad and brother
both died from it."

Has he had a colonoscopy?
No.
Why not?
Thought he would wait till 40,
though doctors recommended it sooner.

I hold his hand as he struggles to
digest this news.
A team of doctors will now
do their best to prolong
some meaningful life for him.

But he and I, in unspoken
understanding,
know his future in this life
is short.

PREVAIL

JULIE

She is cheerleader,
athlete, bright,
16 years popular.
Tiny, size 4.

Today, she has a backache.
When she lies down,
I suddenly see an obvious
advanced pregnancy,
completely hidden
when she stands.

I am surprised!
And even more so to discover
on exam,
this baby is arriving today.

We both go directly to the hospital,
where, shortly, she delivers
a lively 8 pound boy.

Before I leave the room,
she asks to speak.

"Tonight is prom.
Oh please, can I go?"

IN THE WORDS OF JAN THATCHER ADAMS, M.D.

I am flabbergasted
with the whole situation.
Her parents don't yet
even know they are
grandparents.

"I'll be careful,
and come right back to the hospital
at midnight."

I still have the photo of
her in the blue size 4
prom dress that fit perfectly.
I can only imagine the conversations
with her parents
and her not-the-father prom date.

But I see her determination
to continue unfolding
into fulfilled womanhood.
And I see her instant joy
with her supposedly surprise son.

I am witness to a force of nature.

GLORIA

She is in her 80s.
Still walking 2 miles a day.
Today is her yearly visit.

She is in good spirits,
all is fine.
No complaints.

On exam, I find an ugly, green-aging bruise
on her left rib cage.
And no breath sounds in her left lung.

"Oh, that bruise. I fell on the fence
2 weeks ago."

X-ray confirms a completely collapsed
lung and a chest cavity
filled with blood.

Have you been walking every day — 2 miles?
"Sure I have, why not?
Is something wrong?"

This is one tough lady.
I elect to let nature
cure the problem,
and do not place any tubes.

IN THE WORDS OF JAN THATCHER ADAMS, M.D.

2 weeks later-
50% improved.
2 more weeks, x-ray clear.

Good attitude,
good genetics,
good life habits.
Miracle healing.

Terry Moore

Terry Moore has been an avid writer of short stories and poems since childhood. A retired Air Force officer and civil servant, his writings reflect his worldwide travels and his great love of the outdoors.

Originally from Tennessee, Terry admits to travelling to Bacon Rind Creek, Arkansas during the height of the mosquito season. Residing in the Pacific Northwest, he continues to explore its forests and waters, the nature of its creatures, and spirits of those who came before him.

Contact Terry at ironfeather43@gmail.com

IN THE WORDS OF TERRY MOORE

KEEPING YOUR DISTANCE

We sat on the couch in your folks' parlor
Saturday evening last,
my arm draped around your shoulders,
your head warmly cuddled against my cheek,
your hands holding my free hand.
Your folks had gone to the Elks Club spring social
and wouldn't be home for hours.
Your sister was at a sleepover,
your brother on a camping trip.
"Chances Are" was turned low on the radio.

Ten minutes and two dozen more kisses,
and we were breathing hard.
Thirty minutes and hands were exploring,
faces flushed, and there was moaning.
Zippers were down, and we weren't sitting anymore.
Then we stopped, in spite of ourselves.

We don't want a baby . . . yet, he said.
We could walk down to the drugstore, she said,
then realized that the blabby clerk that worked there
would tell anyone who would listen
about the Johnson boy and his steady, buying condoms.

We didn't have sex, but touched each other to climax,
and when we could, again, breathe normally,
we swore love and planned our life after high school.

PREVAIL

We enjoyed our hours on the couch, tickled, and joked.
Too soon her parents returned, and I went home,
after a steamy front porch kiss;
not knowing how long it would have to last.
The next day the corona virus broke out,
and for months we've each had to stay at home,
keeping our distance, while hormones and viruses rage.

OLYMPIC PENINSULA Authors

Founded in 2016, the goal of Olympic Peninsula Authors has been to help writers in our community find each other and to share their work with interested readers. The founders, Heidi Hansen and Linda B. Myers, are dedicated to that goal, even though 2020 has thrown a hitch into our event schedule of readings and workshops. We continue to publish anthologies; Fourth Friday Readings in Sequim now fits under the OPA wing and will continue when the time is right. We launched a YouTube channel (Olympic Peninsula Authors) where local writers read their works. This year, we experimented with publishing books other than the anthologies under the OPA banner.

We are not an association with dues and by-laws and secret hand signals. That may come but for now, we enjoy wandering off to explore new meadows. We covet your ideas and welcome your help.

Copies of *IN THE WORDS OF OLYMPIC PENINSULA AUTHORS*, Volumes 1, 2, and 3 are available through us or Amazon.hastin

Facebook.com/Olympic Peninsula Authors
olympicpeninsulaauthors@gmail.com
P.O. Box 312
Carlsborg, WA 98324

Made in the USA
Columbia, SC
16 November 2020